Heritage Builders®

Proverbs
Family Nights Tool Chest ™

Creating Lasting Impressions for the Next Generation

Jim Weidmann and Del Van Essen
with Kurt Bruner

Faith Parenting™

Cook Communications

I dedicate this book to my helpmate, best friend, and wife, Diane.
Thanks for encouraging me as the spiritual leader of our household.
I also dedicate this book to my four kids, Nicole, Seth, Caleb,
and Chelsea. They keep me creative and active.
I love you,
Del

Chariot Victor Publishing
a division of Cook Communications Ministries, Colorado Springs, Colorado 80918
Cook Communications, Paris, Ontario
Kingsway Communications, Eastbourne, England

HERITAGE BUILDERS™/FAMILY NIGHT TOOL CHEST—PROVERBS™
© 2000 by Jim Weidmann, Del Van Essen, and Kurt Bruner

First edition 2000

Edited by Steve Parolini
Design by Bill Gray
Interior Layout by Pat Miller
Cover and Interior Illustrations by Guy Wolek

ISBN 0-78143-361-4

Printed and bound in the United States of America
04 03 02 01 00   5 4 3 2 1

Heritage Builders/Family Night Tool Chest—Proverbs is a Heritage Builders™ book.
To contact Heritage Builders Association, send email to: Hbuilders@aol.com.

Contents

Family Nights for Proverbs

The Heritage Builders™ Series

This resource was created as an outreach of the Heritage Builders Association—a network of families and churches committed to passing a strong heritage to the next generation. Designed to motivate and assist families as they become intentional about the heritage passing process, this series draws upon the collective wisdom of parents, grandparents, church leaders, and family life experts, in an effort to provide balanced, biblical parenting advice along with effective, practical tools for family living. For more information on the goals and work of the Heritage Builders Association, please see page 110.

Kurt Bruner, M.A.
Executive Editor
Heritage Builders™ Series

Introduction

There is toothpaste all over the plastic-covered table. Four young kids are having the time of their lives squeezing the paste out of the tube—trying to expunge every drop like Dad told them to. "Okay," says Dad, slapping a twenty-dollar bill onto the table. "The first person to get the toothpaste back into their tube gets this money!" Little hands begin working to shove the peppermint pile back into rolled-up tubes—with very limited success.

Jim is in the midst of a weekly routine in the Weidmann home when he and his wife spend time creating "impression points" with the kids. "We can't do it, Dad!" protests the youngest child.

"The Bible tells us that's just like your tongue. Once the words come out, it's impossible to get them back in. You need to be careful what you say because you may wish you could take it back." An unforgettable impression is made.

Impression points occur every day of our lives. Intentionally or not, we impress upon our children our values, preferences, beliefs, quirks, and concerns. It happens both through our talk and through our walk. When we do it right, we can turn them on to the things we believe. But when we do it wrong, we can turn them off to the values we most hope they will embrace. The goal is to find ways of making this reality work for us, rather than against us. How? By creating and capturing opportunities to impress upon the next generation our values and beliefs. In other words, through what we've labeled impression points.

The kids are all standing at the foot of the stairs. Jim is at the top of that same staircase. They wait eagerly for Dad's instructions.

"I'll take you to Baskin Robbins for ice cream if you can figure how to get up here." He has the attention of all four kids. "But there are a few rules. First, you can't touch the stairs. Second, you can't touch the railing. Now, begin!"

After several contemplative moments, the youngest speaks up. "That's impossible, Dad! How can we get to where you are without touching the stairs or the railing?"

After some disgruntled agreement from two of the other children, Jacob gets an idea. "Hey, Dad. Come down here." Jim walks down the stairs. "Now bend over while I get on your back. Okay, climb the stairs."

Bingo! Jim proceeds to parallel this simple game with how it is impossible to get to God on our own. But when we trust Christ's completed work on our behalf, we can get to heaven. A lasting impression is made. After a trip up the stairs on Dad's back, the whole gang piles into the minivan for a double scoop of mint-chip.

Several years ago, Jim and his wife Janet began setting aside time to intentionally impress upon the kids their values and beliefs through a weekly ritual called "family night." They play games, talk, study, and do the things which reinforce the importance of family and faith. It is during these times that they intentionally create these impression points with their kids. The impact? The kids are having fun and a heritage is being passed.

๏ intentional or "oops"?

Sometimes, we accidentally impress the wrong things on our kids rather than intentionally impressing the right things. But there is an effective, easy way to change that. Routine family nights are a powerful tool for creating intentional impression points with our children.

The concept behind family nights is rooted in a biblical mandate summarized in Deuteronomy 6:5-9.

> *"Love the LORD your God with all your heart and with all your soul and with all your strength. These commandments that I give you today are to be upon your hearts. Impress them on your children."*
> ***How?***
> *"Talk about them when you sit at home and when you walk along the road, when you lie down and when you get up. Tie them as symbols on your hands and bind them on your foreheads. Write them on the doorframes of your houses and on your gates."*

In other words, we need to take advantage of every opportunity to impress our beliefs and values in the lives of our children. A

growing network of parents are discovering family nights to be a highly effective, user-friendly approach to doing just that. As one father put it, "This has changed our entire family life." And another dad, "Our investment of time and energy into family nights has more eternal value than we may ever know." Why? Because they are intentionally teaching their children at the wisdom level, the level at which the children understand and can apply eternal truths.

☺ truth is a treasure

Two boys are running all over the house, carefully following the complex and challenging instructions spelled out on the "truth treasure map" they received moments ago. An earlier map contained a few rather simple instructions that were much easier to follow. But the "false treasure box" it led to left something to be desired. It was empty. Boo Dad! They hope for a better result with map number two.

STEP ONE:

Walk sixteen paces into the front family room.

STEP TWO:

Spin around seven times, then walk down the stairs.

STEP THREE:

Run backwards to the other side of the room.

STEP FOUR:

Try and get around Dad and climb under the table.

You get the picture. The boys are laughing at themselves, complaining to Dad, and having a ball. After twenty minutes of treasure hunting they finally reach the elusive "truth treasure box." Little hands open the lid, hoping for a better result this time around. They aren't disappointed. The box contains a nice selection of their favorite candies. Yea Dad!

"Which map was easier to follow?" Dad asks.

"The first one," comes their response.

"Which one was better?"

"The second one. It led to a true treasure," says the oldest.

"That's just like life," Dad shares. "Sometimes it's easier to follow what is false. But it is always better to seek and follow what is true."

They read from Proverbs 2 about the hidden treasure of God's truth and end their time repeating tonight's jingle—"It's best for you to seek what's true." Then they indulge themselves with a mouthful of delicious candy!

the power of family nights

The power of family nights is twofold. First, it creates a formal setting within which Dad and Mom can intentionally instill beliefs, values, or character qualities within their child. Rather than defer to the influence of peers and media, or abdicate character training to the school and church, parents create the opportunity to teach their children the things that matter most.

The second impact of family nights is perhaps even more significant than the first. Twenty to sixty minutes of formal fun and instruction can set up countless opportunities for informal reinforcement. These informal impression points do not have to be created, they just happen—at the dinner table, while driving in the car, while watching television, or any other parent/child time together. Once you have formally discussed a given family night topic, you and your children will naturally refer back to those principles during the routine dialogues of everyday life.

If the truth were known, many of us hated family devotions while growing up. We had them sporadically at best, usually whenever our parents were feeling particularly guilty. But that was fine, since the only thing worse was a trip to the dentist. Honestly, do we really think that is what God had in mind when He instructed us to teach our children? As an alternative, many parents are discovering family nights to be a wonderful complement to or replacement for family devotions as a means of passing their beliefs and values to the kids. In fact, many parents hear their kids ask at least three times per week:

"Can we have family night tonight?"

Music to Dad's and Mom's ears!

⊚ Keys to Effective Family Nights

There are several keys which should be incorporated into effective family nights.

MAKE IT FUN!

Enjoy yourself, and let the kids have a ball. They may not remember everything you say, but they will always cherish the times of laughter—and so will you.

KEEP IT SIMPLE!

The minute you become sophisticated or complicated, you've missed the whole point. Don't try to create deeply profound lessons. Just try to reinforce your values and beliefs in a simple, easy-to-understand manner. Read short passages, not long, drawn-out sections of Scripture. Remember: The goal is to keep it simple.

DON'T DOMINATE!

You want to pull them into the discovery process as much as possible. If you do all the talking, you've missed the mark. Ask questions, give assignments, invite participation in every way possible. They will learn more when you involve all of their senses and emotions.

GO WITH THE FLOW!

It's fine to start with a well-defined outline, but don't kill spontaneity by becoming overly structured. If an incident or question leads you in a different direction, great! Some of the best impression opportunities are completely unplanned and unexpected.

MIX IT UP!

Don't allow yourself to get into a rut or routine. Keep the sense of excitement and anticipation through variety. Experiment to discover what works best for your family. Use books, games, videos, props, made-up stories, songs, music or music videos, or even go on a family outing.

DO IT OFTEN!

We tend to find time for the things that are really important. It is best to set aside one evening per week (the same evening if possible) for family night. Remember, repetition is the best teacher. The more impressions you can create, the more of an impact you will make.

MAKE A MEMORY!

Find ways to make the lesson stick. For example, just as advertisers create "jingles" to help us remember their products, it is helpful to create family night "jingles" to remember the main theme—such as "It's best for you to seek what's true" or "Just like air, God is there!"

USE OTHER TOOLS FROM THE HERITAGE BUILDERS TOOL CHEST!

Family night is only one exciting way for you to intentionally build a loving heritage for your family. You'll also want to use these other exciting tools from Heritage Builders.

The Family Fragrance: There are five key qualities to a healthy family fragrance, each contributing to an environment of love in the home. It's easy to remember the Fragrance Five by fitting them into an acrostic using the word "Aroma"—

A—Affection
R—Respect
O—Order
M—Merriment
A—Affirmation

Family Moments: Ways that we impress on our children our values, preferences, and concerns. We do it through our talk and our actions. We do it intentionally (through such methods as Family Nights), and we do it incidentally.

Family Compass: Family Compass is the standard of normal healthy living against which our children will be able to measure their attitudes, actions, and beliefs.

Family Traditions: Meaningful activities which promote the process of passing on emotional, spiritual, and relational inheritance between generations. Family traditions can play a vital role in this process.

Please see the back of the book for information on how to receive the FREE Heritage Builders Newsletter which contains more information about these exciting tools! Also, look for the new book, *The Heritage*, available at your local Christian bookstore.

⊚ How to Use This Tool Chest

Summary page: For those who like the bottom line, we have provided a summary sheet at the start of each family night session. This abbreviated version of the topic briefly highlights the goal, key Scriptures, activity overview, main points, and life slogan. On the reverse side of this detachable page there is space provided for you to write down any ideas you wish to add or alter as you make the lesson your own.

Step-by-step: For those seeking suggestions and directions for each step in the family night process, we have provided a section which walks you through every activity, question, Scripture reading, and discussion point. Feel free to follow each step as written as you conduct the session, or read through this portion in preparation for your time together.

À la carte: We strongly encourage you to use the material in this book in an "à la carte" manner. In other words, pick and choose the questions, activities, Scriptures, age-appropriate ideas, etc. which best fit your family. This book is not intended to serve as a curriculum, requiring compliance with our sequence and plan, but rather as a tool chest from which you can grab what works for you and which can be altered to fit your family situation.

The long and the short of it: Each family night topic presented in this book includes several activities, related Scriptures, and possible discussion items. Do not feel it is necessary to conduct them all in a single family night. You may wish to spread one topic over several weeks using smaller portions of each chapter, depending upon the attention span of the kids and the energy level of the parents. Remember, short and effective is better than long and thorough.

Journaling: Finally, we have provided space with each session for you to capture a record of meaningful comments, funny happenings, and unplanned moments which will inevitably occur during family night. Keep a notebook of these journal entries for future reference. You will treasure this permanent record of the heritage passing process for years to come.

@1: Proverbial Wisdom

Teaching children the importance of Proverbs

Scripture
• Proverbs 1:1-7

ACTIVITY OVERVIEW		
Activity	Summary	Pre-Session Prep
Activity 1: Cake Bake	Learn how Proverbs is like a recipe for living godly lives.	You'll need ingredients for baking a cake, and a Bible.
Activity 2: Distraction	Learn to focus on God's wisdom as written in Proverbs.	You'll need toothpicks, and a Bible.

Main Points:

—Proverbs teaches us how to live godly lives.

—We must work hard to learn from the Proverbs and gain wisdom.

LIFE SLOGAN: "In Proverbs we find; wisdom of every kind."

Make it your own
In the space provided below, outline the flow and add any additional ideas to guide you through the process of conducting this family night.

Prayer & Praise Items
In the space provided below, list any items you wish to pray about or give praise for during this family night session.

Journal
In the space provided below, capture a record of any fun or meaningful things which happened during this family night session.

Session Tip

We intentionally have provided more material than we would expect to be used in a single "Family Night" session. You know your family's unique interests and life circumstances best, so feel free to adapt this lesson to meet your family members' needs. Remember, short and simple is better than long and comprehensive.

WARM-UP

Open with Prayer: Begin by having a family member pray, asking God to help everyone in the family understand more about Him through this time. After prayer, review your last lesson by asking these questions:

- **What did we learn about in our last lesson?**
- **What was the Life Slogan?**
- **Have your actions changed because of what we learned? If so, how?** Encourage family members to give specific examples of how they've applied learning from the past week.

Share: Today we are going to learn why it's important to study the Book of Proverbs.

ACTIVITY 1: Cake Bake

Point: Proverbs teaches us how to live godly lives.

Supplies: You'll need ingredients for baking a cake, and a Bible.

Activity: Get out the ingredients and supplies for baking a cake. If you have more than one child, prepare enough supplies so each child can work on a cake (or a single layer of a multiple-layer cake). Give each child the appropriate recipe and have them do their best to make a cake. If you have a "made from scratch" recipe for a cake—use this instead of a store-bought mix. Make sure the recipe is clear and easy to follow.

As much as possible, allow your children to bake the cakes by themselves. It's important for this activity that they have the experience of following a recipe.

While the cake is baking consider the following questions:

• **How important was it to have a recipe in order to bake the cake?** (Very important . . . without it I wouldn't know what to do; a recipe helps us do the right thing; without a recipe the cake would taste terrible.)

• **How does a recipe guide you?** (It helps us put in the right amount of ingredients; it tells us how long to bake the cake.)

Share: God has given us instructions to follow in His Word, the Bible. In fact, there is one book that includes instructions or directions written just for young Christians. That book is Proverbs. Proverbs means: to rule or govern. Solomon wrote Proverbs to give us advice that can govern or direct our lives.

 Ask:

• **Now that you've baked a cake, do you think you could do it again?** (Yes, now I know how; I could do better because I've tried it once.)

Share: When you had a recipe in front of you, you had all the knowledge you needed to bake a cake. But once you've baked a cake, now you have the experience of baking a cake too. Proverbs tell us how to apply God's truth to our daily lives—they teach us wisdom.

Read Proverbs 1:1-6. Then **share:** Proverbs is like a recipe book for our lives. It teaches us how to live godly lives and to learn wisdom.

Age Adjustments

YOUNG CHILDREN won't be able to complete this activity without a fair amount of adult supervision. This lessens the value of the activity as it is designed to help children discover the value and importance of following directions. So rather than bake a cake, give younger children instructions to make something more appropriate and fun for their age level. For example, have them make a graham cracker creation by spreading peanut butter on the cracker surface and making a smiling face with marshmallow eyes, chocolate chip nose, and uncooked pasta mouth. This serves the same purpose and leads into a discussion about following instructions.

ACTIVITY 2: Distraction

Point: We must work hard to learn from the Proverbs and gain wisdom.

 Supplies: You'll need toothpicks and a Bible.

Activity: Pour a box of toothpicks onto the floor to be counted. (You could use any small

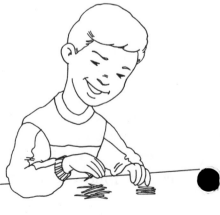

objects such as paper clips, straws, or even candy.) If you have more than one child, send all but one out of the room and have that child begin counting the toothpicks. While your child is counting, call out random numbers to get him or her to lose count. After a few attempts to count the items, call "time." Repeat this activity for each child.

? When all children have attempted this activity, consider the following questions:

- **What was it like to try and count these toothpicks?** (It was hard because I lost count; I had to concentrate in order to count them.)
- **How easy was it to ignore my distractions?** (It was difficult; I couldn't do it; you kept confusing me.)

Read aloud Proverbs 1:7. Then **share: This Scripture passage tells us that fools ignore wisdom and discipline. But if we want to be wise and grow in our understanding of God, we need to work hard at learning wisdom. Proverbs is loaded with great advice and wise thoughts for us to learn. But the world throws us all kinds of distractions to keep us from learning wisdom. Just as it was difficult for you to count the tooth-picks while I distracted you, you will face many distractions as you try to make wise choices. Studying Proverbs can help us make good decisions in all areas of our lives.**

Age Adjustments

OLDER CHILDREN AND TEENAGERS may find the toothpick activity too easy. So, give them an alternative challenge. Have them quote a Bible passage or poem while you distract them in various ways. Or, have them try to solve a complex math problem while you shout random numbers.

WRAP-UP

Gather everyone in a circle and have family members take turns answering this question: **What's one thing you've learned about God today?**

Next, tell kids you've got a new "Life Slogan" you'd like to share with them.

Life Slogan: Today's Life Slogan is this: "In Proverbs we find; wisdom of every kind." Have family members repeat the slogan two or three times to help them learn it. Then encourage them to practice saying it during the week so they can talk about it at your next family night session.

Close in Prayer: Allow time for each family member to share prayer concerns and answers to prayer. Then close your time together with prayer for each concern. Thank God for listening to and caring about us.

Remember to record your prayer requests so you can refer to them in the future as you see God answering them.

2: Facing Temptations

Teaching children the importance of making good decisions when facing temptation

Scripture
• Proverbs 5:1-2, 7-8, 21-23; 6:20-24; 7:1-5

ACTIVITY OVERVIEW

Activity	Summary	Pre-Session Prep
Activity 1: Defending Positions	Learn the importance of guarding against temptation.	You'll need golf balls (or other small balls), a blanket, empty coffee cans, candy, and a Bible.
Activity 2: What Color Is This?	Learn how to fight temptation.	You'll need crayons or markers, paper, and Bibles.

Main Points:
—We must guard our minds against temptation.
—It takes self-discipline to fight temptation.

LIFE SLOGAN: "To guard from sin; let wisdom in."

Make it your own

In the space provided below, outline the flow and add any additional ideas to guide you through the process of conducting this family night.

Prayer & Praise Items

In the space provided below, list any items you wish to pray about or give praise for during this family night session.

Journal

In the space provided below, capture a record of any fun or meaningful things which happened during this family night session.

WARM-UP

Open with Prayer: Begin by having a family member pray, asking God to help everyone in the family understand more about Him through this time. After prayer, review your last lesson by asking these questions:

- **What did we learn about in our last lesson?**
- **What was the Life Slogan?**
- **Have your actions changed because of what we learned? If so, how?** Encourage family members to give specific examples of how they've applied learning from the past week.

Share: Today we are going to learn why it's important to have self-discipline and fight temptations.

ACTIVITY 1: Defending Positions

Point: We must guard our minds against temptation.

Supplies: You'll need golf balls (or other small balls), a blanket, empty coffee cans, candy, and a Bible.

Activity: Set up a play area in your family room by laying a blanket along the ground near a wall. This will be used as a "bumper" pad to keep the golf balls from denting or otherwise harming the baseboard.

Give a child two coffee cans (or similar-sized containers—bowls work just fine too). This child will be the "defender." Have the defender stand in front of the blanket-protected wall. Then give each family member a supply of golf balls (or similar-sized balls—Ping-Pong balls work just as well, though they are harder to roll).

Explain that the goal of the defender is to trap as many balls as possible before they hit the blanketed wall. Tell him or her that there is a reward for each ball caught in the cans. Tell other family members they're to roll the balls quickly to try and reach the blanket. On your signal, begin the game. Keep the defender busy by rolling the balls rapidly toward the wall.

It is likely he or she won't be able to stop all (or even most) of the balls rolled.

After playing this game, award one piece of candy to the defender for each ball he or she caught in the cans. Repeat the activity so each family member gets a chance to play (yes, Mom and Dad too!).

Age Adjustments

YOUNG CHILDREN may have some difficulty understanding the concept of "temptation." To help them with this, place a favorite candy on a table and ask them to look at it—but not to touch it. Younger children will know what it's like to want the candy even though they were told not to touch it. You can then use this feeling to help them see what a temptation is. Use lots of examples they can relate to during the activity. For example, you might talk about the temptation to lie; the temptation to call someone a mean name; or the temptation to take more candy than they were offered.

After picking up the balls, place them in the cans and sit in a circle around them. Consider the following questions:

• **What was it like to try and catch all these balls?** (It was impossible; it wasn't easy; I could only catch some of them.)

• **If we imagine these golf balls are temptations, how is this activity like real life?** (We face lots of temptations; temptations come at us faster than we can react sometimes.)

Have family members take turns picking out one golf ball from the can and sharing a temptation they have faced. Continue until each family member has shared at least two or three temptations (or until the cans are empty).

Share: As we can see, we face many temptations in our lives. But the Bible gives us good advice for guarding against temptation.

Read aloud Proverbs 5:1-2, 7-8, 21-23. Then ask:
• **What do these verses tell us about temptation?** (When we understand God's Word we can fight temptation; we need to work hard to avoid the world's temptations.)
• **How do we discipline ourselves?** (Stay away from things that might be bad for us; read the Bible; choose friends who will be a good influence.)

Share: When we were trying to guard the wall from the golf balls, we only had two cans to help us. In our everyday lives, we sometimes feel like we're losing the battle with temptation too. But when we study the

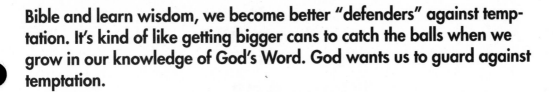

Bible and learn wisdom, we become better "defenders" against temptation. It's kind of like getting bigger cans to catch the balls when we grow in our knowledge of God's Word. God wants us to guard against temptation.

ACTIVITY 2: What Color Is This?

Point: It takes self-discipline to fight temptation.

 Supplies: You'll need crayons or markers, paper, and Bibles.

Activity: Send the children out of the room while you prepare this next activity. Write a color name (blue, green, yellow, etc.) on a sheet of paper, using a different color crayon or marker and a different color sheet of paper for each word. Mix up the colors so they don't match. For example, you might write the word "blue" on a yellow sheet of paper using a green crayon. Create five or six of these mixed-up color sheets. Then invite one child in at a time to play the game.

Explain to your child that you're going to flash a sheet of paper at him or her and that he or she is to tell you the color of the word written on that paper. Quickly flash the papers, allowing just a glimpse of them before flipping them face down on the table. Then ask your child to recall the words that were on each sheet of paper. Award one point for each correct word color and for each recalled word. Then repeat the activity for the other children.

 Consider these discussion questions:
- **Was it easy to do this activity? Why or why not?** (No, the colors and words don't match; I didn't get to see the words for long.)
- **Were you tempted to say the word rather than the color? Why or why not?** (Yes, because it was confusing; no, I stayed focused on the color of the word.)

 Read aloud Proverbs 6:20-24 and 7:1-5. Ask:
- **What do these truths tell us?** (We need to work hard to obey God; we need to know God's Word.)

Share: Just as it took discipline and careful thinking to call out the color of the words rather than the words themselves, it takes discipline to overcome temptations and guard against sin. We can grow discipline by reading the Bible; reciting verses in our minds when we're facing

temptation; sharing verses or truths with others who are in need; and considering what Jesus would do in our situation. We can learn to focus on what's right and ignore the bad influences that lead to sin.

Age Adjustments

YOUNG CHILDREN who can't read yet will need a slight adjustment to make this activity work. Simply place a few strips of different-color paper on a sheet of yet another paper color. When you flash the papers, have children identify and call out the color of the middle paper strip. This can still be a challenge for younger children as their eyes will be directed to multiple colors on the paper.

WRAP-UP

Gather everyone in a circle and have family members take turns answering this question: **What's one thing you've learned about God today?**

Next, tell kids you've got a new "Life Slogan" you'd like to share with them.

Life Slogan: Today's Life Slogan is this: "To guard from sin; let wisdom in." Have family members repeat the slogan two or three times to help them learn it. Then encourage them to practice saying it during the week so they can talk about it at your next family night session.

Close in Prayer: Allow time for each family member to share prayer concerns and answers to prayer. Then close your time together with prayer for each concern. Thank God for listening to and caring about us.

Remember to record your prayer requests so you can refer to them in the future as you see God answering them.

3: Honesty

Teaching children the importance of being honest

Scripture
- Proverbs 6:16-19; 11:1; 12:13, 19
- Exodus 20:16

ACTIVITY OVERVIEW		
Activity	**Summary**	**Pre-Session Prep**
Activity 1: Tipped Scales	Learn that God hates dishonesty.	You'll need small candies (like M&Ms), rubber bands, large serving spoons, a cloth napkin, a marker, and a Bible.
Activity 2: Pebble in My Shoe	Learn how lying eats away at our hearts and minds.	You'll need small pebbles, eggs, a spoon, and a Bible.

Main Points:

—The truth is a delight to God.

—Dishonesty teaches others to distrust us.

LIFE SLOGAN: "Delight God in what you say; tell the truth every day."

Make it your own

In the space provided below, outline the flow and add any additional ideas to guide you through the process of conducting this family night.

Prayer & Praise Items

In the space provided below, list any items you wish to pray about or give praise for during this family night session.

Journal

In the space provided below, capture a record of any fun or meaningful things which happened during this family night session.

Session Tip

We intentionally have provided more material than we would expect to be used in a single "Family Night" session. You know your family's unique interests and life circumstances best, so feel free to adapt this lesson to meet your family members' needs. Remember, short and simple is better than long and comprehensive.

WARM-UP

Open with Prayer: Begin by having a family member pray, asking God to help everyone in the family understand more about Him through this time. After prayer, review your last lesson by asking these questions:

- **What did we learn about in our last lesson?**
- **What was the Life Slogan?**
- **Have your actions changed because of what we learned? If so, how?** Encourage family members to give specific examples of how they've applied learning from the past week.

Share: Today we are going to learn why God values honesty.

ACTIVITY 1: Tipped Scales

Point: The truth is a delight to God.

 Supplies: You'll need small candies (like M&Ms), rubber bands, large serving spoons, a cloth napkin, a marker, and a Bible.

Activity: Before starting this activity, have children put on mismatched socks. Don't explain why until prompted to in the second activity.

Then prepare a simple "scale" by using a rubber band to connect two equal-sized serving spoons at the handle. Tape a fat marker (or similar-sized cylindrical object) onto your table, and cover it with a cloth napkin. Place as many M&Ms as you can onto one of the spoons. These will be your share of the candy. Then place the spoon scale onto the marker, adjusting its location so the fulcrum (center of balance) is closer to your share. [See illustration.]

This will create a situation where the other side of the scale will require fewer M&Ms in order to be balanced. The object of this activity is to illustrate dishonesty in the form of "tipping the scales in your favor." That's why your goal is to create an uneven balance—with fewer candies required on the empty spoon for the scale to be balanced.

One at a time, have children enter the room. Explain that they'll be able to have as much candy as it takes to balance the scale. Then help them place the candies on the uneven scale until the spoons balance. Kids will probably notice right away that the scale isn't fairly balanced. Acknowledge that they may be right, but continue with the activity until candies are weighed and given to your child. Repeat the activity for each child.

Age Adjustments

YOUNG CHILDREN will connect best with this activity if you can help them relate to examples of dishonesty they might encounter daily. For example, young children sometimes don't tell the whole truth about whether or not they brushed their teeth; or prefer to disguise the truth when they've done something wrong (broken a lamp, played with a sibling's toy without permission, etc.). Use specific examples they can relate to from their own experience to help drive home the point that dishonesty is a bad thing.

Then get together and consider these questions:
- **Why didn't you get as much candy as you saw on the opposite spoon?** (The balance wasn't fair; you cheated.)
- **What are other experiences you've had where things just didn't seem fair?** (Answers will vary.)

Read Proverbs 6:16-19; 11:1; and Exodus 20:16. Then ask:
- **According to these passages, what does God hate?** (Dishonesty; lying; cheating.)

Share: In the candy scale activity you were not given a fair deal. That's because I had rigged the scale to allow more candy on my side of the scale than on yours. This is an example of dishonesty or lying. God despises lying. In fact, He hates it so much, He made it one of the 10 Commandments.

Most of us know what it's like to be tempted to lie. What are some of the things you've been tempted to be dishonest about? (Answers will vary, but be sure to add a few of your own temptations.)

Read aloud Proverbs 12:19. **Share: God delights when we tell the truth. Before we speak, we should think carefully if what we're going to say is truthful. That way, we'll always delight God with our words.**

ACTIVITY 2: Pebble in My Shoe

Point: Dishonesty teaches others to distrust us.

 Supplies: You'll need small pebbles, eggs, a spoon, and a Bible.

 **Activity:** Have each family member put a small stone in one of their shoes until it is under their foot. Have them stand and share what it feels like to have a pebble in their shoe. Then have them go outside (or into a room where spills can be easily cleaned up). Set up a simple starting and ending point for a race. Give each family member a spoon. Then place an egg in each spoon and have family members race from the starting point to the finish line while carrying the egg in the spoon. Race until you have a winner (or until all eggs have been dropped). Then form a circle and discuss the following question:

- **How did it feel to race with a pebble in your shoe?** (It didn't feel good; I couldn't go as fast.)

Read Proverbs 12:13. Then **share: Dishonesty and lying traps us—just as the pebble was trapped in your shoe. We can't out-run our lies, they stick close to us. Eventually, if we lie too many times, people stop trusting us. Then it takes a long time to rebuild that trust.**

Have family members look at their mismatched socks. **Share: When we are dishonest, our words don't match our actions—just as our socks don't match. And just like we don't always see our socks, we can't always tell when someone is being dishonest. Yet, at the end of the day—you'll notice your socks don't match. Likewise, eventually people will discover our dishonesty. With God's help, we can choose to match our good words with good actions—so we can be trusted by others.**

WRAP-UP

Gather everyone in a circle and have family members take turns answering this question: **What's one thing you've learned about God today?**

Next, tell kids you've got a new "Life Slogan" you'd like to share with them.

Life Slogan: Today's Life Slogan is this: "Delight God in what you say; tell the truth every day." Have family members repeat the slogan two or three times to help them learn it. Then encourage them to practice saying it during the week so they can talk about it at your next family night session.

 Close in Prayer: Allow time for each family member to share prayer concerns and answers to prayer. Then close your time together with prayer for each concern. Thank God for listening to and caring about us.

Remember to record your prayer requests so you can refer to them in the future as you see God answering them.

☉ 4: Humility

Teaching children the difference between pride and humility

Scripture
• Proverbs 11:2; 13:10; 15:33; 16:5, 18, 19; 18:12; 29:23

ACTIVITY OVERVIEW		
Activity	Summary	Pre-Session Prep
Activity 1: A Qualities Puzzle	Learn the difference between humility and pride.	You'll need a handout cut and marked as indicated in the activity (see illustration) and a Bible.
Activity 2: Stamping Out Pride	Learn why it's important to stamp out pride and hold onto humility.	You'll need 3X5 cards, markers, and a Bible.

Main Points:
   —A humble heart pleases God.
   —We should stamp out pride in our lives.

LIFE SLOGAN: "Stamp out pride and keep humility on your side."

Make it your own

In the space provided below, outline the flow and add any additional ideas to guide you through the process of conducting this family night.

Prayer & Praise Items

In the space provided below, list any items you wish to pray about or give praise for during this family night session.

Journal

In the space provided below, capture a record of any fun or meaningful things which happened during this family night session.

Session Tip

We intentionally have provided more material than we would expect to be used in a single "Family Night" session. You know your family's unique interests and life circumstances best, so feel free to adapt this lesson to meet your family members' needs. Remember, short and simple is better than long and comprehensive.

 WARM-UP

Open with Prayer: Begin by having a family member pray, asking God to help everyone in the family understand more about Him through this time. After prayer, review your last lesson by asking these questions:

- **What did we learn about in our last lesson?**
- **What was the Life Slogan?**
- **Have your actions changed because of what we learned? If so, how?** Encourage family members to give specific examples of how they've applied learning from the past week.

Share: Today we are going to learn the value of humility.

ACTIVITY 1: A Qualities Puzzle

Point: A humble heart pleases God.

Supplies: You'll need a handout cut and marked as indicated in the activity (see illustration) and a Bible.

Activity: Copy the model of the letter "H" on page 34. Before cutting out the shapes, write one word that might describe a humble person in each of the spaces. Here are a few words you might use: modest, meek, courteous, respectful, submissive, thankful, helpful, kind. Then cut out the puzzle pieces and write on the opposite side of each piece a word describing a prideful person. These could include words such as: conceited, selfish, vain, arrogant, boastful, mean, bossy.

Shuffle the puzzle pieces and place them on a table. Invite children to try and put the "H"

Age Adjustments

OLDER CHILDREN AND TEENAGERS can help you create the "H" puzzle by coming up with the words to include on either side. Ask them to come up with words describing both humble and prideful attitudes. Then use these to complete the "H" puzzle. You can then use this puzzle with younger children who didn't come up with the words, but will discover their meaning as they attempt to put together the puzzle. Older children can help put the puzzle together once the other family members have determined which words match.

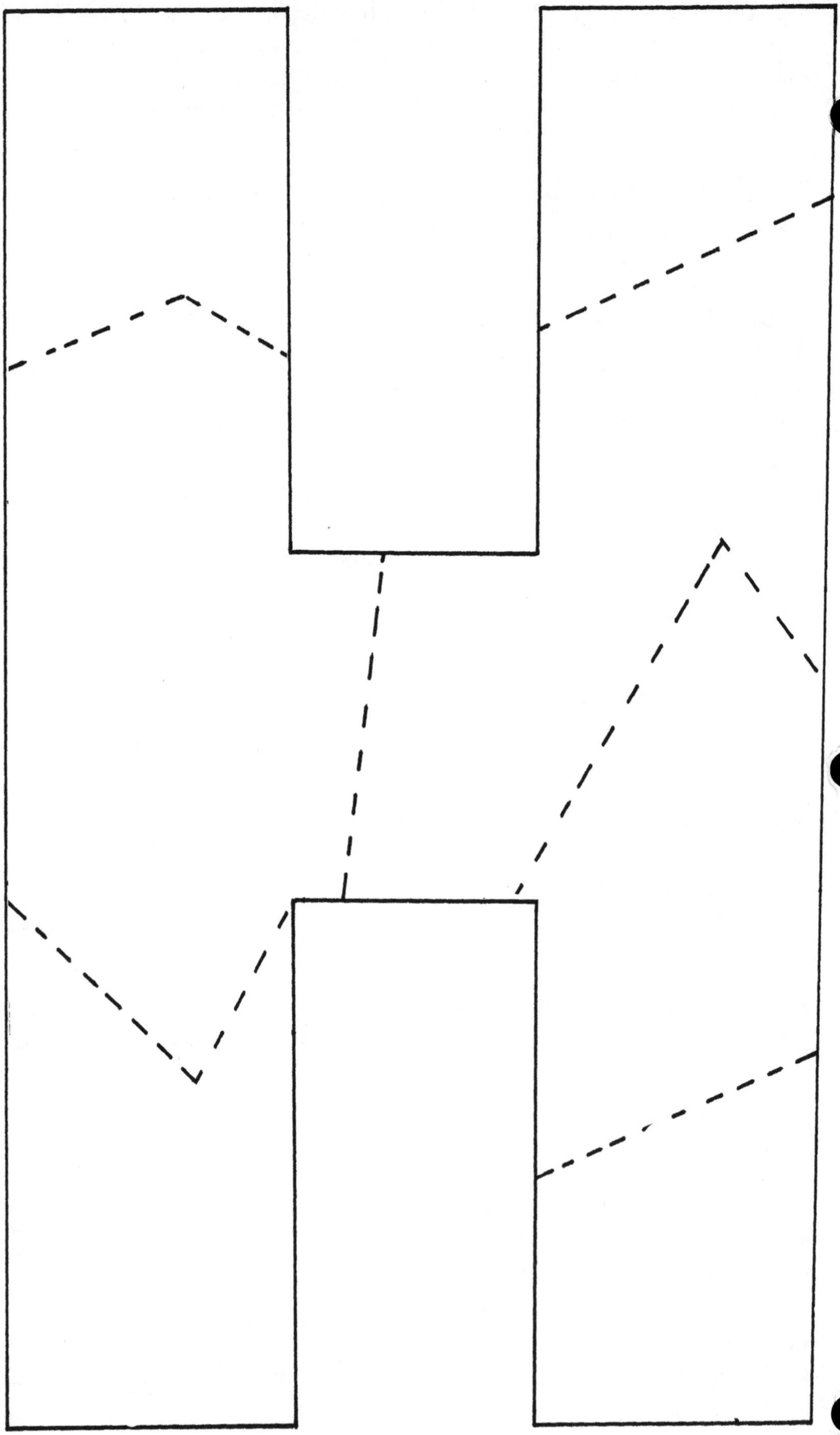

together. Explain that the first thing they need to do is to figure out which words on the puzzle pieces match—so they can place them right-side up and complete the puzzle. If children need a hint, suggest that they have only the words that represent humility or the words that represent pride turned face up. Once they have all the matching words, it will be possible to create the "H."

Note: For younger children, pre-draw a simple "H" within the outline on the side with the humility words before cutting it out of the handout. This will guide them to make the right choice when placing the pieces on the table.

When kids have completed the "H," you may ask them to compare the words on either side of the puzzle.

 Ask:
- **What kinds of people do the words on each side describe?** (Someone who is humble; someone who is prideful or boastful.)

Share: The letter "H" was used for this activity because it is the first letter in the word humility. A humble person has the traits listed on one side of this puzzle. A humble person doesn't brag; lets others go first in line; serves others.

 Read Proverbs 15:33; 16:5, 18; and 29:23. Then discuss the following questions:
- **What do these verses tell us about humility and pride?** (Pride is a bad thing; we should be humble.)
- **What are some examples of being humble?** (Saying "thank you" when you're told something nice, but not boasting about it; allowing someone else to be first in line or to get the biggest piece of pie.)
- **What are some examples of being prideful?** (Boasting about a test grade; telling someone how smart you are just to make that person feel bad.)

Share: We all struggle with pride. It's really easy to start boasting when we're with friends and we want to impress them. But God wants us to have humble hearts.

ACTIVITY 2: Stamping Out Pride

Point: We should stamp out pride in our lives.

 Supplies: You'll need 3X5 cards, markers, and a Bible.

Activity: Write the following six results of pride and six results of humility each on a separate 3X5 card or sheet of paper:

RESULTS OF PRIDE:	RESULTS OF HUMILTY:
• Leads to shame	• Leads to wisdom
• Encourages quarrels	• Listens to advice
• Disliked by friends	• Brings honor and respect
• Leads to punishment	• Brings contentment and freedom
• Ends in a downfall	• Ends in honor
• God hates this	• Receives grace

NOTE: You may find it necessary to select different words/phrases for younger children.

Shuffle the cards and place them face down on the floor, one to two feet apart in a rectangular grid arranged in three rows and four columns. Have family members take turns flipping over two cards each. If a card is a result of pride, have the child stamp on it and keep his or her foot on the card. If the card lists a result of humility, have them "hold onto humility" by placing their hand on it. Repeat until family members are tangled up in a "Twister-like" arrangement on the floor.

 While family members are still twisted up on the floor, consider these questions:

• **What do the cards at your feet say about the results of pride?** (Have family members read their stomped-out cards.)
• **What do the cards under your hands say about the results of humility?** (Have family members grab their cards, stand, and read them aloud.)

Share: Just as you stomped on the results of pride, we must stamp out pride in our lives. God wants us to grab onto humility and be good examples for others with our humble hearts.

 Read aloud Proverbs 11:2; 13:10; 16:19; and 18:12. Then have children paraphrase these passages in their own words.

Share: The results of humility are wisdom and honor. Let's do our best

to choose humility instead of pride as we relate to our friends, family members, and others.

WRAP-UP

Gather everyone in a circle and have family members take turns answering this question: **What's one thing you've learned about God today?**

Next, tell kids you've got a new "Life Slogan" you'd like to share with them.

Life Slogan: Today's Life Slogan is this: "Stamp out pride and keep humility on your side." Have family members repeat the slogan two or three times to help them learn it. Then encourage them to practice saying it during the week so they can talk about it at your next family night session.

Close in Prayer: Allow time for each family member to share prayer concerns and answers to prayer. Then close your time together with prayer for each concern. Thank God for listening to and caring about us.

Remember to record your prayer requests so you can refer to them in the future as you see God answering them.

5: Wisdom and Foolishness

Teaching children the difference between being wise and foolish

Scripture
• Proverbs 1:3, 4-7; 10:13, 21; 12:11; 14:15-16; 15:14, 21; 16:16, 22; 17:10; 19:25; 29:8, 11

ACTIVITY OVERVIEW		
Activity	**Summary**	**Pre-Session Prep**
Activity 1: Different Paths	Learn how life can be easier if you follow wisdom.	You'll need paper cups, a 4-foot-long 2X4, a food prize, and a Bible.
Activity 2: One Step at a Time	Learn how wisdom is gained in little "bite-sized" pieces.	You'll need a big box, lots of heavy books, and a Bible.

Main Points:

—The road of the foolish is hard; the road of the wise has rewards.

—We must work hard to become wise one step at a time.

LIFE SLOGAN: "The foolish doubt; the wise search out."

Make it your own
In the space provided below, outline the flow and add any additional ideas to guide you through the process of conducting this family night.

Prayer & Praise Items
In the space provided below, list any items you wish to pray about or give praise for during this family night session.

Journal
In the space provided below, capture a record of any fun or meaningful things which happened during this family night session.

WARM-UP

Open with Prayer: Begin by having a family member pray, asking God to help everyone in the family understand more about Him through this time. After prayer, review your last lesson by asking these questions:

• **What did we learn about in our last lesson?**
• **What was the Life Slogan?**
• **Have your actions changed because of what we learned? If so, how?** Encourage family members to give specific examples of how they've applied learning from the past week.

Share: Today we are going to learn the value of wisdom in our lives.

ACTIVITY 1: Different Paths

Point: The road of the foolish is hard; the road of the wise has rewards.

Supplies: You'll need paper cups, a 4-foot-long 2X4, a food prize, and a Bible.

Activity: You'll want to do this activity outside if at all possible. If weather prohibits you from outdoor activity, simply replace the water with marbles (if you're doing this on a carpeted floor) or small rubber balls (if you're doing this on a non-carpeted floor). You would also need to place obstacles (such as small blocks or other items) on the floor for the second part of this activity if you do it indoors.

Have your child take off his or her shoes and socks. Hand the child a 2X4 board that's about 4 feet long to hold out in front of him or her. [See illustration.] Place a Styrofoam cup filled with water on each end of the board for your child to balance. Then have your child walk across smooth ground (grass or sidewalk) for about 20 feet without letting the cups tip or fall. Repeat the activity, but have your child walk across a rough surface (such as gravel, or an area that's been littered with pebbles or small rocks). Make sure all children get a chance to try this balancing game at least once.

Age Adjustments

YOUNG CHILDREN who haven't yet developed fine motor skills may have difficulty with this activity. You can simplify it by using a broom handle instead of a board, and by hanging baskets with marbles or candy in them instead of cups of water. This will allow them to be successful while still providing a bit of a challenge.

After everyone's tried this balancing game at least once, form a circle and discuss the following questions:

• **How easy or difficult was it to balance the water (or marbles) as you walked?** (It was tough; I didn't have any trouble with it; I thought it was hard.)

• **Which path was easier to travel?** (The smooth one.)

• **If you could do this game over and walk down just one path, which would you choose?** (The grass or carpet.)

Share: Just as your feet felt both smooth and bumpy ground during this activity, there are similar contrasts in life. Proverbs teaches us that the foolish lifestyle is like walking on rocks or bumpy ground and that the wise lifestyle is like walking on smooth ground like grass or carpet.

Have family members look up and **read** the following Scriptures, then call out characteristics of foolish and wise people, based on the content of the Scriptures: Proverbs 10:21; 14:15-16; 15:14; 16:16, 22; 17:10; 19:25; 29:8, 11. Here are some of the possible conclusions:

Foolish people . . .
     . . . lack judgment
     . . . are gullible
     . . . are arrogant and careless
     . . . receive punishment
     . . . stir up anger.
Wise people . . .
     . . . seek knowledge
     . . . value wisdom over riches
     . . . respond to correction
     . . . control their anger
     . . . help others with good advice.

After family members have finished this activity, **share: Proverbs often compares wise and foolish people. And just as you discovered in this activity, the road of the foolish person is hard and full of pain and troubles. The road of the wise person is much smoother (though it still takes work, just as you still had to balance the cups of water or marbles).**

ACTIVITY 2: One Step at a Time

Point: We must work hard to become wise one step at a time.

 **Supplies:** You'll need a big box, lots of heavy books, and a Bible.

Activity: Place a large box on one side of a room and fill it with large, heavy books. Make sure you have enough books in the box so it is impossible to lift. List the following thoughts on separate sheets of paper and tape them to random books in the box:

- Be willing to receive instruction (Proverbs 1:3)
- Have a listening ear (Proverbs 1:5-6)
- Trust and receive God (Proverbs 1:7)
- Be willing to accept correction (Proverbs 19:25)
- Take responsibility for your own actions (Proverbs 12:11)
- Be humble
- Pray
- Seek help from Christian friends and teachers

Bring one child in at a time and ask them to move the books from one side of the room to the other. They'll quickly discover the impossibility of moving the box all at once. When they learn to move a few books at a time, they'll be able to succeed. Have children read the notes attached to books as they move them from one side of the room to the other. When the books have been moved, then redeposited into the box, have other children repeat the activity.

When everyone's had a chance to move the books, consider these questions:
- **What did you learn about moving the box of books?** (I couldn't do it all at once; I had to move small amounts at a time.)
- **How is this like the way we grow in wisdom?** (We grow little by little; we don't get wisdom in one huge chunk.)

Share: The results of growing wise include controlling your anger (Proverbs 29:11); being admired as counselors (Proverbs 10:13); staying on straight paths (Proverbs 15:21); and much more. Wise people avoid bad paths.

Have family members take turns sharing about examples of foolishness and wise behavior they've witnessed. Then **share: When we work step by step at becoming wise, we please God and gain many rewards. But when we choose the path of foolishness, we stumble and fall. It is a good thing to grow in wisdom by studying God's Word, going to church, praying, and participating in family night activities like this one!**

WRAP-UP

Gather everyone in a circle and have family members take turns answering this question: **What's one thing you've learned about God today?**

Next, tell kids you've got a new "Life Slogan" you'd like to share with them.

Life Slogan: Today's Life Slogan is this: "The foolish doubt; the wise search out." Have family members repeat the slogan two or three times to help them learn it. Then encourage them to practice saying it during the week so they can talk about it at your next family night session.

Close in Prayer: Allow time for each family member to share prayer concerns and answers to prayer. Then close your time together with prayer for each concern. Thank God for listening to and caring about us.

Remember to record your prayer requests so you can refer to them in the future as you see God answering them.

☺ 6: The Tongue

Teaching children that the words they say can be used for good or evil

Scripture
• Proverbs 6:16-19; 11:13; 13:14; 15:4; 16:24; 18:21; 27:6

ACTIVITY OVERVIEW		
Activity	**Summary**	**Pre-Session Prep**
Activity 1: Sour Taste	Learn how the words we say can damage others.	You'll need lemon slices, glasses of water, and a Bible.
Activity 2: Encouraging Words	Learn the importance of encouraging one another.	You'll need colorfully decorated boxes, stickers, paper, pens or pencils, and a Bible.

Main Points:

—Sour words can hurt other people.

—It is a good thing to say encouraging words.

LIFE SLOGAN: "Love is sent through encouragement."

Make it your own
In the space provided below, outline the flow and add any additional ideas to guide you through the process of conducting this family night.

Prayer & Praise Items
In the space provided below, list any items you wish to pray about or give praise for during this family night session.

Journal
In the space provided below, capture a record of any fun or meaningful things which happened during this family night session.

Session Tip

We intentionally have provided more material than we would expect to be used in a single "Family Night" session. You know your family's unique interests and life circumstances best, so feel free to adapt this lesson to meet your family members' needs. Remember, short and simple is better than long and comprehensive.

WARM-UP

Open with Prayer: Begin by having a family member pray, asking God to help everyone in the family understand more about Him through this time. After prayer, review your last lesson by asking these questions:

- **What did we learn about in our last lesson?**
- **What was the Life Slogan?**
- **Have your actions changed because of what we learned? If so, how?** Encourage family members to give specific examples of how they've applied learning from the past week.

Share: Today we are going to learn how the words we say can help or hurt each other.

ACTIVITY 1: Sour Taste

Point: Sour words can hurt other people.

Supplies: You'll need lemon slices, glasses of water, and a Bible.

Activity: Have everyone sit together around a table. Hand lemon slices to each family member (you'll need one too!). Then, at the very same time, have each person put a lemon slice in their mouth. See who can keep it there for 30 seconds. While you're doing this, have family members look around at each other and enjoy the sour faces.

After 30 seconds (or longer, if you have a few brave souls in your family), remove the lemon slices and offer each person a drink of water.

Note: Your children may enjoy this activity even more if you use sour candies instead of lemons. Your children can probably tell you about the candy that ranks as the sourest of the bunch. Consider having some of this on hand even if you use the lemons—it makes a great reminder for children to choose words that aren't sour. (You can hand it out after the activity if you like.)

 After time is up, discuss the following questions:

- **What were you thinking as you sucked on the lemon?** (I didn't like it; I wanted to spit it out; it tasted terrible.)
- **How can words be like the sour lemon taste?** (They can be mean words; they can make you feel bad.)
- **What kinds of words do people say that leave a sour taste in their mouths?** (Mean words; hateful words; cursing; things that make people want to cry.)

Share: When people lie (Proverbs 6:16-19); when people use bad language (Proverbs 15:4); and when people gossip (Proverbs 11:13); it "sours" their relationship with others—just as the lemon made our taste buds sour. God wants us to avoid saying things that can hurt other people. Instead, He wants us to use words that are helpful and sweet.

ACTIVITY 2: Encouraging Words

Point: It is a good thing to say encouraging words.

Supplies: You'll need colorfully decorated boxes, stickers, paper, pens or pencils, and a Bible.

Activity: Before the activity, decorate shoe boxes with colorful wrapping paper (you'll need one for each family member). Use gold or silver foil paper if possible—or some other shiny paper that looks jewel-like. Set a supply of colorful stickers on a table. (Look for stickers that offer encouraging messages such as "You're Great!" or "Nice Work," and stickers that represent the different interests of your children.) Then hide the boxes around the house in various locations (the dryer, a closet, behind a chair, etc.).

Gather family members together around the table. **Share: Each person here has a special "Good Words" box hidden somewhere in the house. You can go searching for it now, or you can earn clues to** find the box. You earn one clue for each kind thing you say to someone around this table. After you have a clue, you must try to find the box. If you can't, return and get another clue by saying something nice to another family member.

As family members say kind things, give them clues to direct them to their boxes. Start your clues with general directions (such as: it's on this floor of the house, or it's inside something) and make them more specific each time a family member returns for another.

When everyone's found his or her box, return to the table and have family members decorate each other's boxes. Then have family members sign their boxes (a permanent marker works well on this kind of wrapping paper). When the boxes are complete, set them aside and **read** aloud Proverbs 16:24; 27:6; and 13:14. Consider these questions:

- **These verses tell us about the positive power of words. What are some good ways we can use our tongues?** (Encourage each other; tell the truth; tell others about Jesus.)
- **What are some ways we've been doing this today?** (Answers will vary.)
- **How do you feel when someone says kind things to you?** (It makes me feel good; I feel special.)
- **Describe a time someone gave you encouraging words. What happened? How did you feel?** (Answers will vary.)

Share: Proverbs tells us "death and life are in the power of the tongue" (Proverbs 18:21). That's a pretty powerful statement. Our words can be harmful or helpful. These boxes we've decorated are going to be used for helpful words. Whenever you want to say something kind, write a simple note to that person and put it in his or her box. Let's try to say something nice to each family member at least once a week—or more often! You can check inside your box whenever you want and read encouraging words.

Note: You'll need to keep the boxes in a place that's accessible to all family members (such as a family room). You'll also need to be the leader in this activity and make sure to put a note in each child's box at least once a week. If

Age Adjustments

YOUNG CHILDREN who don't yet know how to write can simply draw pictures and place them in the boxes to show how much they care for family members. Or, they can put small toys or other objects in the boxes as a gesture of kindness.

You may even want to teach younger children who are nearly ready to read and write how to write such simple words as "love" and "smile." Then they can write their own notes and feel a certain satisfaction of their own as well as encouraging a sibling.

you can do this daily, the impact will be even greater and you'll be modeling the kind of positive behavior that will help children be encouragers of others.

Close your activity time by having each person write his or her first note to each family member.

WRAP-UP

Gather everyone in a circle and have family members take turns answering this question: **What's one thing you've learned about God today?**

Next, tell kids you've got a new "Life Slogan" you'd like to share with them.

Life Slogan: Today's Life Slogan is this: "Love is sent through encouragement." Have family members repeat the slogan two or three times to help them learn it. Then encourage them to practice saying it during the week so they can talk about it at your next family night session.

Close in Prayer: Allow time for each family member to share prayer concerns and answers to prayer. Then close your time together with prayer for each concern. Thank God for listening to and caring about us.

Remember to record your prayer requests so you can refer to them in the future as you see God answering them.

@ 7: God's Plan

Teaching children how to discover God's plan for their lives

Scripture
• Proverbs 13:13; 15:29; 22:17-19; 24:10; 27:21; 29:25

ACTIVITY OVERVIEW		
Activity	Summary	Pre-Session Prep
Activity 1: Point of Power	Learn why it's important to stay close to our source of power, God.	You'll need a wooden 6- to 12-inch dowel 1/4-inch in diameter, construction paper, tape, and a Bible.
Activity 2: Straight and True	Learn how God points us toward His plan for our lives.	You'll need construction paper, tape, glue, and a Bible.

Main Points:
—Prayer keeps us connected to God.
—God points us toward His plan.

LIFE SLOGAN: "Be just like the arrow—straight and true; for God has a plan just for you."

Make it your own

In the space provided below, outline the flow and add any additional ideas to guide you through the process of conducting this family night.

Prayer & Praise Items

In the space provided below, list any items you wish to pray about or give praise for during this family night session.

Journal

In the space provided below, capture a record of any fun or meaningful things which happened during this family night session.

Session Tip

We intentionally have provided more material than we would expect to be used in a single "Family Night" session. You know your family's unique interests and life circumstances best, so feel free to adapt this lesson to meet your family members' needs. Remember, short and simple is better than long and comprehensive.

WARM-UP

Open with Prayer: Begin by having a family member pray, asking God to help everyone in the family understand more about Him through this time. After prayer, review your last lesson by asking these questions:

- **What did we learn about in our last lesson?**
- **What was the Life Slogan?**
- **Have your actions changed because of what we learned? If so, how?** Encourage family members to give specific examples of how they've applied learning from the past week.

Share: Today we are going to learn how prayer can help us discover God's plan for our lives.

ACTIVITY 1: Point of Power

Point: Prayer keeps us connected to God.

Supplies: You'll need a wooden 6- to 12-inch dowel 1/4-inch in diameter, construction paper, tape, and a Bible.

Activity: Place the supplies on a table and introduce the theme of today's family night. Then have children each begin creating an arrow according to the following instructions:

Cut a small strip of construction paper and wrap it around one end of the dowel, allowing some of the paper to extend off of the end of the dowel (see illustration). Tape the paper in place and cut a notch in the paper. This will become the end of the arrow that rests against the bow's string.

When each family member has completed this part of the arrow construction, consider the following questions:

- **What is the purpose of the notch on this arrow?** (It holds the arrow on the string; it is what the archer holds onto.)
- **How would the arrow work if it didn't have a notch?** (It wouldn't be easy to control; it would fly wildly.)

Share: The notch on the arrow has many purposes. But one of the most important is that this is the place where the power is transferred into the arrow. It's where the arrow gets its energy to fly off toward a target.

Age Adjustments

OLDER CHILDREN AND TEENAGERS will better "connect" with the point of this activity if they get a chance to actually shoot an arrow at a target. Arrange ahead of time to go to an archery range for a simple lesson and practice time. During this archery practice, children will actually experience the power of the bow and how the notch in the arrow is critical for its flight distance and accuracy. You can then make the leap to compare this critical factor to the critical factor of prayer and how it is necessary to give us good direction and purpose in life.

Read aloud Proverbs 15:29. Then discuss these questions:

- **What does this passage say about the wicked and the righteous?** (Wicked people are far from God; righteous people are connected to God.)
- **How do we stay connected to God?** (By praying; listening to Him; by reading the Bible.)
- **How is prayer like the notch in the arrow?** (They both keep things connected; they're both the place where you get power.)

Share: Just as the notch connects the arrow to the bow, prayer keeps us connected to God. The place where the arrow gets its power is its notch; just as the place where we get our power is through prayer. Prayer keeps us connected to God. Spending time with God allows us to discover God's will for our lives.

ACTIVITY 2: Straight and True

Point: God points us toward His plan.

 Supplies: You'll need construction paper, tape, glue, and a Bible.

Activity: Have children continue the creation of their arrows. Help them cut three rectangles as in the illustration. Use glue or tape to attach the rectangles to the dowel near the notch as illustrated. This will create the "feathers" for the arrows. Children may then cut slits in the rectangles to make them look more like feathers.

 As the feathers begin to dry, consider the following question:
- **What is the purpose of these feathers?** (They make the arrow fly straighter; they help direct the arrow.)

Read Proverbs 13:13. Then ask:
- **Where has God given us instructions for life?** (In the Bible.)

Share: Just as the feathers guide the arrow, God's Word can guide our lives through all the decisions we must make.

Have children decorate the shaft of the arrow with markers. Then **share: The shaft of the arrow gives it strength and integrity. In Proverbs 24:10 and 27:21 we learn what integrity means. We learn that we need to believe in God and stand by our beliefs no matter what the situation. Since God will never leave or forsake us, we can count on Him to help us have strength and integrity.**

Have children finish their arrows by creating a point out of two equal-sized triangles and attaching them to the front end of the dowel. Ask children to tell you the purpose of the arrow's point. Then **read** Proverbs 22:17-19 and 29:25.

 Consider these questions:
- **What is the point of these verses?** (Trust God.)
- **What should be our "target" in life?** (To trust God; to grow closer to God.)

Share: We need to be full of integrity (as the arrow's shaft is full of integrity); learn God's path for us by reading the Bible (as the feathers lead the arrow to its target); and stick to God's promises (just as the arrow's point holds it to the target).

Have children place their arrows in a prominent place in their rooms as a reminder to pray, study God's Word, trust God, and hold fast to God's promises as they discover His will for their lives.

WRAP-UP

Gather everyone in a circle and have family members take turns answering this question: **What's one thing you've learned about God today?**

Next, tell kids you've got a new "Life Slogan" you'd like to share with them.

Life Slogan: Today's Life Slogan is this: "Be just like the arrow—straight and true; for God has a plan just for you." Have family members repeat the slogan two or three times to help them learn it. Then encourage them to practice saying it during the week so they can talk about it at your next family night session.

Close in Prayer: Allow time for each family member to share prayer concerns and answers to prayer. Then close your time together with prayer for each concern. Thank God for listening to and caring about us.

Remember to record your prayer requests so you can refer to them in the future as you see God answering them.

8: God's Plan for Work

Teaching children that hard work is pleasing to God

Scripture
• (Various Proverbs)

ACTIVITY OVERVIEW		
Activity	Summary	Pre-Session Prep
Activity 1: Unpopped	Learn the value of "doing your best work" by partially popping some popcorn.	You'll need microwave popcorn and a microwave (or supplies for popping corn on the stovetop) and a Bible.
Activity 2: Working for Candy	Learn the rewards of working hard by knocking candy out of a pinata.	You'll need a pinata (or supplies to make one—see activity), a broomstick, and a Bible.

Main Points:

—God doesn't like laziness.

—Work as unto the Lord.

LIFE SLOGAN: "Laziness will make you poor; God's glory is what work is for."

Make it your own

In the space provided below, outline the flow and add any additional ideas to guide you through the process of conducting this family night.

Prayer & Praise Items

In the space provided below, list any items you wish to pray about or give praise for during this family night session.

Journal

In the space provided below, capture a record of any fun or meaningful things which happened during this family night session.

WARM-UP

Open with Prayer: Begin by having a family member pray, asking God to help everyone in the family understand more about Him through this time. After prayer, review your last lesson by asking these questions:

- **What did we learn about in our last lesson?**
- **What was the Life Slogan?**
- **Have your actions changed because of what we learned? If so, how?** Encourage family members to give specific examples of how they've applied learning from the past week.

Share: Today we are going to learn why God values hard work.

ACTIVITY 1: Unpopped

Point: God doesn't like laziness.

Supplies: You'll need microwave popcorn and a microwave (or supplies for popping corn on the stovetop) and a Bible.

Activity: Tell your children you'd like to start the family night by making some popcorn. Get a bag of microwave popcorn and let it pop for about half of its intended time. Once you hear the popcorn kernels begin to pop, wait just a few seconds and turn off the microwave. (Similarly, if you use the stovetop to pop the popcorn, allow just a few kernels to pop before quitting.)

Your children will probably begin to complain that you didn't wait long enough. That's the idea! Pour the popcorn into a bowl, making sure kids see the unpopped kernels as well as the ones they'll get to eat. Enjoy the popped kernels together while you discuss the following questions:

• **What did you think when we didn't get much popcorn from this bag?** (I was disappointed; you should have popped it longer; I didn't get much popcorn.)
• **Did I do the popcorn popping job right?** (No, you didn't let it go long enough; no, you were impatient.)

Age Adjustments

YOUNG CHILDREN may not understand the concept of laziness because they're always "on the go." You can help them see this trait by pointing out specific ways they might be lazy (such as cleaning up a room or eating vegetables). Help them to see that laziness means not doing something that is important to do or waiting too long to do it.

Share: We were disappointed when the popcorn didn't get completely cooked. I was impatient when I stopped the popping before it was done. In a similar way, God is disappointed when we only do part of the work that should be done; or when we are impatient and take "short cuts" in our work. I was lazy.

Read the following Proverbs and have family members share characteristics of a lazy person: Proverbs 22:13 (gives excuses for not working); 6:9 (has trouble getting started); 13:4, 21:25 (never carries out ideas); 18:9 (is unproductive); 12:27 (is a quitter); 20:17; 11:18 (deceives others).

Then **read** the following passages and have family members brainstorm the results of laziness: Proverbs 10:4; 14:23 (can't pay bills/becomes poor); 15:19 (has troubles in life); 19:15 (goes hungry); 10:5 (misses harvest time).

Share: If you were working for a big company and did nothing all day, you'd soon be out of a job. Laziness is displeasing to employers . . . and to parents. But all of us must watch and be good workers in life, because laziness is most displeasing to God.

Return to the kitchen and pop a full bag (or pot) of popcorn. Enjoy this together as you move into the next activity.

ACTIVITY 2: Working for Candy

Point: Work as unto the Lord.

Supplies: You'll need a pinata (or supplies to make one—see activity), a broomstick, and a Bible.

Activity: Attach a pinata to a string and hang it in a safe place outdoors (where kids will have plenty of room to swing a broom handle in the air). If you can't buy a pinata, make one of your own. Simply fill a paper grocery sack with newspaper and candy and tie the top of the bag closed.

Note: You may want to have one pinata for each child.

When the pinata is prepared, blind-fold your child and give him or her a few spins in place. Then hand your child a broom handle and watch as he or she works to break open the pinata. Rotate so all children get a chance to break the pinata (or repeat the activity so each child breaks his or her own pinata).

Share: It took a lot of effort or work to break open the pinata. Sometimes you were swinging at the air and missed the pinata altogether. Other times, you hit the pinata but it didn't break. That's how we're to be in life too. Though we aren't blindfolded in real life, sometimes it may feel like it! Still, God wants us to work hard to complete things. He wants us to be hard workers. And just as you got some candy for your hard work, there are rewards for us when we are good workers in everyday life (though the reward may be in heaven and not on earth).

 Consider these questions:
- **What kinds of workers would you want if you ran an amusement park?** (Hard workers; people who did what they were told.)
- **What are the benefits of being a hard worker?** (You feel good about yourself; you get more done; people like you.)

Share additional benefits from the following Proverbs: Proverbs 28:19 (reap abundance); 22:29 (honored by your boss); 12:14 (get rewards); 13:4 (will be satisfied).

Have family members suggest practical ways they can show their desire to work hard. This could include: clear the dishes whether asked or not; pick up your room; get school work done right away before playing; practice musical instruments or sports to improve that skill).

 Read Proverbs 6:6-8. Ask family members to tell what this passage says about working hard.

Share: If we follow the example of the ant, we'll be good planners. We

are to work hard, not to get lots of money or be famous, but to serve God. Colossians 3:23 tells us "Whatever you do, work at it with all your heart, as working for the Lord, not for men."

WRAP-UP

Gather everyone in a circle and have family members take turns answering this question: **What's one thing you've learned about God today?**

Next, tell kids you've got a new "Life Slogan" you'd like to share with them.

Life Slogan: Today's Life Slogan is this: "Laziness will make you poor; God's glory is what work is for." Have family members repeat the slogan two or three times to help them learn it. Then encourage them to practice saying it during the week so they can talk about it at your next family night session.

Close in Prayer: Allow time for each family member to share prayer concerns and answers to prayer. Then close your time together with prayer for each concern. Thank God for listening to and caring about us.

Remember to record your prayer requests so you can refer to them in the future as you see God answering them.

9: A Teachable Heart

Teaching children the importance of having a teachable heart

Scripture
• Proverbs 12:15; 13:18; 15:31; 25:12; 29:1

ACTIVITY OVERVIEW		
Activity	Summary	Pre-Session Prep
Activity 1: Captain, May I?	Learn what it means to be teachable by following instructions during a game.	You'll need a "medal" for each family member (see lesson) and a Bible.
Activity 2: Moldable	Learn how to be moldable.	You'll need supplies for making play dough (flour, alum, salad oil, salt, boiling water), and a Bible.

Main Points:

—It takes work to have a teachable heart.

—God wants us to be moldable.

LIFE SLOGAN: "If we want to be usable; we must become teachable."

Make it your own
In the space provided below, outline the flow and add any additional ideas to guide you through the process of conducting this family night.

Prayer & Praise Items
In the space provided below, list any items you wish to pray about or give praise for during this family night session.

Journal
In the space provided below, capture a record of any fun or meaningful things which happened during this family night session.

Session Tip

We intentionally have provided more material than we would expect to be used in a single "Family Night" session. You know your family's unique interests and life circumstances best, so feel free to adapt this lesson to meet your family members' needs. Remember, short and simple is better than long and comprehensive.

WARM-UP

Open with Prayer: Begin by having a family member pray, asking God to help everyone in the family understand more about Him through this time. After prayer, review your last lesson by asking these questions:
- **What did we learn about in our last lesson?**
- **What was the Life Slogan?**
- **Have your actions changed because of what we learned?**
  If so, how? Encourage family members to give specific examples of how they've applied learning from the past week.

Share: Today we are going to learn why God wants us to have a teachable heart.

ACTIVITY 1: Captain, May I?

Point: It takes work to have a teachable heart.

Supplies: You'll need a "medal" for each family member (see lesson) and a Bible.

Activity: Before this lesson, prepare a fun, colorful medal for each family member. Write the family member's name and "Teachable Heart" on the medals and attach them to string, yarn, or a chain so they can be worn around the neck.

Open the family night by playing a version of "Captain, May I?" Have family members stand on one side of the room while you stand opposite them. Set a bunch of obstacles and distractions in the room (such as a blaring radio and television; toys and other objects strewn on the floor). Give instructions to individual family members so they can take steps toward you. To do this, call out a family member's name, then give him or her something to do, such as: take five baby steps; give everyone a hug, then move three giant steps closer; and so on. Make your actions fun and positive. The family member must then say "Captain, may I?" before performing the action. If the family member doesn't ask, he or she must return to the beginning place near the wall. After a couple rounds, complicate the game by requiring family members to alternate saying "Captain, may I?" and "May I, Captain?" Again, have family members return to the beginning if they forget to ask or ask using the wrong phrase.

Play until each family member reaches you. (You may want to give easy-to-follow instructions if some kids are having a difficult time with this game.) Present your medals to each family member as they finish the game.

After presenting the medals, consider these questions:
- **What did you like best about this game?** (It was fun; I liked following directions; I got a medal.)
- **What did you like least about this game?** (It was hard; I kept forgetting to say "Captain, May I?")
- **What made this game easy or difficult?** (It was hard because I couldn't remember what to say; it was easy, because I figured out how to play.)

Age Adjustments

YOUNG CHILDREN can play the Captain, may I? game with little difficulty. Be sure to keep their interest up by suggesting unusual and fun actions for them to perform. On the other hand, older children and teenagers may find this game a bit simplistic. To give them more of a challenge, introduce three or four possible "May I" questions that must alternate each time they are called upon. This will elevate the challenge while retaining the flavor of the game and the focus of the activity.

Share: The more you played this game, the better you got at following the directions. It probably wasn't much fun to go back to the beginning, but it's kind of like that in our everyday lives too. It takes work, practice, and something called "discipline" to learn and grow. You each had a "teachable" heart because you learned to play the game better with each turn. That's the way God wants us to be with our hearts as we learn to love Him and love others.

Read aloud Proverbs 25:12; 12:15; 15:31; and 13:18. Have family members summarize the rewards of having a teachable heart as outlined in these passages.

Then **share: Our heart usually wants to do wrong things. But with God's help, we can learn to have a teachable heart—a heart that pleases God.**

ACTIVITY 2: Moldable

Point: God wants us to be moldable.

 Supplies: You'll need supplies for making play dough (flour, alum, salad oil, salt, boiling water), and a Bible.

Activity: Invite family members to join you in making two batches of play dough. For the first batch, place 2 cups of flour, 2 tablespoons of alum, 3 tablespoons of salad oil, and 1 cup of salt into a mixing bowl. Mix thoroughly. Then carefully add 1 cup of boiling water to the dry ingredients and stir until blended. This will form a moldable dough. As you're finishing up the first batch, begin a second batch using the same procedure, but adding an extra cup of flour to the mix. This will create a dry and not very usable dough. You'll need both for the rest of the activity.

Place both kinds of dough on the table. Have children take turns attempting to mold each batch into a ball, dog, cube, or another shape of their choice.

 After each person has worked with both kinds of dough, consider the following questions:

- **What did you notice about these two types of dough?** (One was too dry; one was easy to work with.)
- **Which dough would you prefer to work with?** (The moist one; the one that is moldable.)
- **Imagine that you're play dough. Which kind do you think God would want you to be?** (The moldable kind, because God wants us to do what He asks; the soft one, so we could do things right.)

Read aloud Proverbs 29:1. Then **share: The dough that was too dry just fell apart. If we have a "hard heart" we'll be just like that dry clay. Our lives will fall apart and God will be sad about our choices. But if we have a moldable or a teachable heart, God will be happy because we can learn what God wants us to think, to say, or to do from the Bible and from good Christian leaders like your parents and your Sunday School teacher. God wants us to be like the soft, moldable clay.**

WRAP-UP
Gather everyone in a circle and have family members take turns answering this question: **What's one thing you've learned about God today?**

Next, tell kids you've got a new "Life Slogan" you'd like to share with them.

Life Slogan: Today's Life Slogan is this: "If we want to be usable; we must become teachable." Have family members repeat the slogan two or three times to help them learn it. Then encourage them to practice saying it during the week so they can talk about it at your next family night session.

Close in Prayer: Allow time for each family member to share prayer concerns and answers to prayer. Then close your time together with prayer for each concern. Thank God for listening to and caring about us.

Remember to record your prayer requests so you can refer to them in the future as you see God answering them.

10: Godly Relationships

Teaching children what it means to have godly relationships

Scripture
• Proverbs 11:24; 14:21; 17:9, 17; 27:17

ACTIVITY OVERVIEW		
Activity	Summary	Pre-Session Prep
Activity 1: Clearer Picture	Learn how friends can build one another up.	You'll need candles, matches, construction paper, a black permanent marker, tape, and a Bible.
Activity 2: Tools	Learn how they are like tools in God's toolbox.	You'll need a box of tools and a Bible.

Main Points:

— Friends sharpen one another by being loyal, unselfish, willing to learn, and forgiving.

— God loves it when we use the gifts He's given us to help others.

LIFE SLOGAN: "Be a true friend; love to the end."

Make it your own
In the space provided below, outline the flow and add any additional ideas to guide you through the process of conducting this family night.

Prayer & Praise Items
In the space provided below, list any items you wish to pray about or give praise for during this family night session.

Journal
In the space provided below, capture a record of any fun or meaningful things which happened during this family night session.

Session Tip

We intentionally have provided more material than we would expect to be used in a single "Family Night" session. You know your family's unique interests and life circumstances best, so feel free to adapt this lesson to meet your family members' needs. Remember, short and simple is better than long and comprehensive.

WARM-UP

Open with Prayer: Begin by having a family member pray, asking God to help everyone in the family understand more about Him through this time. After prayer, review your last lesson by asking these questions:

- **What did we learn about in our last lesson?**
- **What was the Life Slogan?**
- **Have your actions changed because of what we learned? If so, how?** Encourage family members to give specific examples of how they've applied learning from the past week.

Share: Today we are going to learn what it means to have godly relationships with our friends.

ACTIVITY 1: Clearer Picture

Point: Friends sharpen one another by being loyal, unselfish, willing to learn, and forgiving.

 Supplies: You'll need candles, matches, construction paper, a black permanent marker, tape, and a Bible.

Activity: Using a black permanent marker, write "Jesus" on a dark piece of construction paper and tape it on one wall of a room that can easily be darkened. You may need to do this activity at night or in a basement where all lights can be turned off. It's important that the room be completely dark. Place a few other candles around the room, near the "Jesus" sign.

Before entering the room with the "Jesus" sign, give each family member a candle. Light the candles, turn off the lights, and walk together into the room with the sign. As you draw nearer to the sign ask children to read it. Then have children help you light the other candles in the room.

When candles are lit, find a place to sit near the sign. Collect the children's candles, if necessary, for safety. Then consider the following questions:

- **What happened to the sign as we got closer to it?** (It became easier to read; it became clearer; it lit up.)
- **How did the letters become sharper?** (The more light we had, the sharper they were; it took lots of candlelight for us to be able to read the sign.)

 Read aloud Proverbs 17:17 and 17:9. Then ask:

- **What do these verses tell us about friends?** (Friends should be there in good and bad times; friends should be loyal; friends should encourage each other; friends should stand up for each other; friends should be willing to forgive.)

Share: As we went closer to the sign, it became sharper. The more lights we added, the easier it was to see. The same is true with our friends. When we help our friends grow closer to Jesus, we sharpen each other—just as the lights made the sign sharper. We sharpen each other by standing up for friends, encouraging them, forgiving them, and being there in good and bad times. Our friendships should be more than just playtimes—they should be growing-closer-to-God times.

 Read Proverbs 27:17. Then ask:

- **What does this verse tell us about friends?** (Friends should listen to one another; friends should hold each other accountable.)
- **What does it mean to hold each other accountable?** (To make sure we're doing the right thing; to support each other and be honest about things.)

Age Adjustments

YOUNG CHILDREN who don't yet read won't be able to identify the word "Jesus" on your sign. Consider taping up a picture of a family member or someone else they'd recognize instead. Then, as young children come closer and more light is thrown on the picture, they'll be able to call out what they see in the picture.

Share: Just as the multiple lights sharpened our picture of Jesus, friends sharpen one another by being loyal, unselfish, willing to learn, and forgiving.

ACTIVITY 2: Tools

Point: God loves it when we use the gifts He's given us to help others.

 Supplies: You'll need a box of tools and a Bible.

Activity: Get a box of tools and place it on the floor. Be sure the toolbox includes a variety of tools—everything from a saw and hammer to screwdrivers and drills. Have children face away from the toolbox. Begin to describe one of the tools. Tap it and demonstrate its sound, if possible. Ask children to guess the tool as soon as they think they know it. Repeat the activity for a number of the tools.

Then have children turn around and look at the tools. Ask them to tell which tool they think they're most like and why. For example, someone might say: I'm like the saw because I'm sharp and I cut right to the point. After everyone has had a turn, **share: Each tool has a very important role. Could I hammer a nail with this saw? Could I cut through wood with this screwdriver? Nope. We all have toolboxes too. But our toolboxes aren't used for building houses or fixing sinks. God gives us a toolbox for relating to friends.**

  Read Proverbs 11:24 and 14:21. Ask:

- **What thoughts do you have about how these tools might relate to being a friend?** (God wants us to reach out to friends . . . and we need tools to do that; the tools God gives us help us help others.)
- **What tools has God given us to help others?** (Friendship; love; patience; concern; caring.)
- **How do we show God's love with the tools He's given us?** (We use the tool of sharing to share toys; we use the tool of friendliness to make a new friend; we use the tool of love to tell others about Jesus.)

Share: God has given us many tools we can use to help others and be good friends. Just like the tools in this box, if we don't use them they rust.

Have family members think of special ways they can help others and reach out to friends using the tools God's given them.

WRAP-UP
Gather everyone in a circle and have family members take turns answering this question: **What's one thing you've learned about God today?**

Next, tell kids you've got a new "Life Slogan" you'd like to share with them.

Life Slogan: Today's Life Slogan is this: "Be a true friend; love to the end." Have family members repeat the slogan two or three times to help them learn it. Then encourage them to practice saying it during the week so they can talk about it at your next family night session.

Close in Prayer: Allow time for each family member to share prayer concerns and answers to prayer. Then close your time together with prayer for each concern. Thank God for listening to and caring about us.

Remember to record your prayer requests so you can refer to them in the future as you see God answering them.

⊚ 11: Success

Teaching children what the Bible says about success

Scripture
• Proverbs 12:3; 13:5; 19:8; 22:4; 25:27; 27:2; 28:12

ACTIVITY OVERVIEW		
Activity	Summary	Pre-Session Prep
Activity 1: High Places	Learn what the world says about success as child is raised on a board.	You'll need a sturdy board or table leaf, a blindfold, and a Bible.
Activity 2: Ears for Success	Learn the importance of listening to instructions during a game.	You'll need cotton balls, a bowl or glass, spoons, and a Bible.

Main Points:

—Money and worldly accomplishments don't make us successful in God's eyes.

—We are successful in God's eyes when we are faithful to obey His instruction.

LIFE SLOGAN: "Fame and fortune seem like success; but without God they make a mess."

Make it your own
In the space provided below, outline the flow and add any additional ideas to guide you through the process of conducting this family night.

Prayer & Praise Items
In the space provided below, list any items you wish to pray about or give praise for during this family night session.

Journal
In the space provided below, capture a record of any fun or meaningful things which happened during this family night session.

Session Tip

We intentionally have provided more material than we would expect to be used in a single "Family Night" session. You know your family's unique interests and life circumstances best, so feel free to adapt this lesson to meet your family members' needs. Remember, short and simple is better than long and comprehensive.

WARM-UP

Open with Prayer: Begin by having a family member pray, asking God to help everyone in the family understand more about Him through this time. After prayer, review your last lesson by asking these questions:

- **What did we learn about in our last lesson?**
- **What was the Life Slogan?**
- **Have your actions changed because of what we learned? If so, how?** Encourage family members to give specific examples of how they've applied learning from the past week.

Share: Today we are going to learn what the Bible teaches us about success.

ACTIVITY 1: High Places

Point: Money and worldly accomplishments don't make us successful in God's eyes.

Supplies: You'll need a sturdy board or table leaf, a blindfold, and a Bible.

Activity: Set the board or table leaf in the middle of a large open space. Place cushions or blankets around the board. Have one child at a time enter the room, blindfolded. Have the child stand on the board or table leaf. Have one parent kneel near either end of the board. (An older sibling may take the place of one of the parents if necessary.) Ask your child to place his hands on top of the parents' heads. Then have the child begin to name people who've been quite successful (past or present). This could include sports stars; actors; singers; and other public figures. Carefully lift the child a few inches off the ground. Then for each name the child gives, have both parents lower their heads just a bit (in unison, if possible). This will give the child the illusion that he or she is being lifted up higher with every name.

After the child has named lots of people and your heads are as low as possible while still able to hold the board off the ground, ask the child to jump off the board. (Assure his safety so he'll be bold enough to try.) If he's been fooled into thinking he was high up in the air, he'll probably fall onto the floor because he has the wrong perception of his distance from the ground.

 Repeat this activity for all children. Then form a circle and discuss the following questions:

- **What did it feel like to be on the board?** (I felt like I was being lifted higher each time I said a name; it was scary.)
- **What did the people you mentioned have in common?** (They all had money; they were all powerful; they were well known.)
- **How is the way you were raised on the board like the way these people are given a "high place" in our society?** (They think they're higher than they really are; it's scary being popular; they're fooling themselves.)
- **What kinds of things does our world say are important for success?** (Money; power; achievements; being famous.)
- **How long do these things last?** (A short time; they could last a long time.)

Age Adjustments

YOUNG CHILDREN may be afraid to stand on the board and be lifted (or may not have the balancing ability to do so). Have these children sit on the board (you'll need to hold it a bit higher to begin with). Then, as they name successful people (or even just their favorite television characters, if they're unfamiliar with what it means to be successful according to the world), you can replicate the same illusion by lowering your head.

You may want to tell about successful people who've fallen on hard times or who've gotten in trouble to emphasize the temporary nature of the world's success. Older children would benefit from a quick history lesson on the devastating power of the stock market plunge that led to the Great Depression. This can quickly put proper perspective on the relative instability of wealth, power, and accomplishment.

 Read Proverbs 12:3; 25:27; and 27:2. Have family members share insights from these verses. Then **share: Money, power, accomplishments, and being famous aren't in God's recipe for success. Just as you thought you were higher than you really were in our opening activity, those people who claim to be successful are really not so high after all. That's because God has a different measure of success.**

ACTIVITY 2: Ears for Success

Point: We are successful in God's eyes when we are faithful to obey His instruction.

 Supplies: You'll need cotton balls, a bowl or glass, spoons, and a Bible.

Activity: Set a bowl on a table at one end of your room. At the opposite end of the room, place a supply of cotton balls and a few spoons. Designate a "starting line" near these supplies. Tell children that they're to fill the bowl with cotton balls as quickly as possible—but they must follow these rules:

1. Begin at the starting line.
2. Hold the spoon out in front of you.
3. Place a cotton ball in the spoon.
4. Walk to the bowl and drop the cotton ball into the bowl. If you drop the ball, return to the starting line and begin again.
5. Go back to the starting line after each cotton ball is dropped and repeat the activity until the bowl is filled.

On your signal, begin the race. Grab a spoon and join in!

  After the bowl is filled, **read** aloud Proverbs 28:12; 13:5; 22:4; and 19:8. Then ask:

• **What do these verses tell us about what makes people successful or what gives them a good reputation?** (A righteous life; telling the truth; being humble; obeying God; reading the Bible.)

• **If we imagine each cotton ball was one of these qualities, how was our game like real life?** (Success takes lots of different things; it takes time and work to be successful; we must take care of things like the truth and obeying God.)

Share: To be successful in the race, we had to listen to instructions and follow them closely. And we had to be determined to go back and forth to fill the bowl. It took time, careful thought, and a focus on the goal. It is the same with God's view of success. We need to be faithful in obeying God's instruction (as written in the Bible), and we need to be diligent or determined to reach the goal of a life that pleases God. When we seek these things and we are faithful to God, we are successful in God's eyes.

Have family members tell ways they can be successful in their relationships with others according to God's view of success. For example, they might say: "I can be successful in God's eyes when I reach out to a friend and help him;" or "I can be successful in God's eyes if I pray often and read the Bible for guidance."

WRAP-UP

Gather everyone in a circle and have family members take turns answering this question: **What's one thing you've learned about God today?**

Next, tell kids you've got a new "Life Slogan" you'd like to share with them.

Life Slogan: Today's Life Slogan is this: "Fame and fortune seem like success; but without God they make a mess." Have family members repeat the slogan two or three times to help them learn it. Then encourage them to practice saying it during the week so they can talk about it at your next family night session.

Close in Prayer: Allow time for each family member to share prayer concerns and answers to prayer. Then close your time together with prayer for each concern. Thank God for listening to and caring about us.

Remember to record your prayer requests so you can refer to them in the future as you see God answering them.

12: Fearing God

Teaching children what it means to fear God

Scripture
• Proverbs 28:14 and selected verses

ACTIVITY OVERVIEW		
Activity	**Summary**	**Pre-Session Prep**
Activity 1: In a Bottle	Learn how people put God "in a bottle."	You'll need an empty wine bottle and cork, a cloth napkin, and a Bible.
Activity 2: Running Away	Learn how to fear God in the right way as they try out a science experiment.	You'll need a bowl, water, pepper, soft soap, and a Bible.

Main Points:

    —God is greater than we can understand; yet He reveals Himself to us through His Word.

    —Fearing God means being in awe of Him and respecting Him.

LIFE SLOGAN: "Hold God in fear and He'll draw near."

Make it your own
In the space provided below, outline the flow and add any additional ideas to guide you through the process of conducting this family night.

Prayer & Praise Items
In the space provided below, list any items you wish to pray about or give praise for during this family night session.

Journal
In the space provided below, capture a record of any fun or meaningful things which happened during this family night session.

Session Tip

WARM-UP

Open with Prayer: Begin by having a family member pray, asking God to help everyone in the family understand more about Him through this time. After prayer, review your last lesson by asking these questions:

- **What did we learn about in our last lesson?**
- **What was the Life Slogan?**
- **Have your actions changed because of what we learned? If so, how?** Encourage family members to give specific examples of how they've applied learning from the past week.

Share: Today we are going to learn what it means to fear God.

ACTIVITY 1: In a Bottle

Point: God is greater than we can understand; yet He reveals Himself to us through His Word.

Supplies: You'll need an empty wine bottle and cork, a cloth napkin, and a Bible.

Activity: For this activity, you'll need an empty wine bottle and a cork. You can usually get these free from a local restaurant. Be sure to wash the bottle and cork before beginning the activity. (You may also be able to find a bottle of nonalcoholic apple cider that uses a cork. This will work as well.)

Hand the bottle to your children and ask them to push the cork into the bottle without breaking it. This won't be easy, and may require a little help from Mom or Dad. Once the cork is in the bottle, ask children to remove it in one piece. They will soon discover the difficulty of this. After allowing time for kids to think up any plan they can for getting the cork out, tell kids you'll show them how it can be done.

1. Take the cloth napkin and feed one corner of it into the bottle so it lays flat on the inside of the bottle. Leave just enough outside the bottle to hold onto.
2. Carefully shake the bottle until the cork is aligned with the opening and is resting on its side on the cloth.
3. Pull slowly to start the cork up the neck of the bottle.
4. Pull hard (and quickly) and the cork should come out of the bottle with the cloth.

 Then set the bottle on the table and discuss the following questions:

- **Which was easier, getting the cork into the bottle or getting it out?** (Getting it in, because we knew how to do that.)
- **How easy would it be to keep track of this cork if we left it in the bottle?** (It would be really easy; we wouldn't lose it because the bottle would be easy to find.)

Share: It's pretty easy to get a cork into a bottle. People do something similar with God! When we think we know everything about God—or when we think we know how He will respond to every situation, we call that "putting God in a bottle." People do that because then they have an easy answer to every situation in life. And they think it's always easy to know what God will do, because His answers are as easy to find as the bottle. But the Bible tells us we can't put God in a bottle. The Bible tells us that we can never fully understand God. It tells us to fear Him. That doesn't mean to be scared of God, but to recognize that we don't know everything about Him.

 Ask:

- **If we can't fully understand God, how do we get to know Him?** (By reading the Bible; by praying; by allowing the Holy Spirit to guide us.)

Share: God tells us about Himself in the Bible. And we can learn a lot about Him by reading Proverbs. We're going to do that now . . . to get to know God better. That way, we'll continue to grow in our understanding of God and will keep from putting Him "in a bottle."

 Read the following glimpses of God by reading the listed passages and pointing out what those verses teach us about God:

84

Proverbs 15:3—God knows everything that happens.
Proverbs 15:11; 16:2; 21:2—God knows the hearts of His people.
Proverbs 16:33; 21:30—God controls all things.
Proverbs 18:10—God is a place of safety.
Proverbs 11:8, 21—God rescues us from danger.
Proverbs 11:31—God condemns the wicked.
Proverbs 15:8, 29—God loves our prayers.
Proverbs 15:9; 22:12—God loves those who obey Him.
Proverbs 15:25; 22:22-23—God cares for the poor and needy.
Proverbs 17:3—God purifies hearts.
Proverbs 17:5; 21:27; 28:9—God hates evil.

 After exploring these glimpses of God, discuss the following questions:

- **What can we learn about God from these passages and other passages in the Bible?** (We can learn that God loves us; we can learn what God would want us to do in life; we can learn how God wants to care for us.)

Share: We can always learn more about God. Because we'll never be able to figure out everything about Him, we should fear Him or show Him respect for His "greatness." God is awesome and should be given honor.

ACTIVITY 2: Running Away

Point: Fearing God means being in awe of Him and respecting Him.

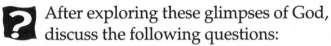 **Supplies:** You'll need a bowl, water, pepper, soft soap, and a Bible.

Activity: If your family enjoys singing, sing the chorus to "Awesome God" together before continuing with this activity.

 Then ask:
- **What does the word "awesome" mean?** (Answers will vary.)
- **In what ways is God awesome?** (He is big; He is powerful; He is the creator of the world; He is everywhere.)

Take a big bowl of water and cover the surface with pepper. Explain

Age Adjustments

YOUNG CHILDREN probably won't be able to push the cork into the bottle for this activity. You can simply demonstrate the activity for younger children if you like. But you could also do a similar activity with a large-mouth jar and a favorite blanket or stuffed animal. When younger children see the large item stuffed into the jar they'll be intrigued on how something so big can fit into something so small. This would be a great lead-in to the discussion about how we can't put God (someone who is bigger than we can imagine) into a box we create (our expectations of Him).

that the pepper represents people. Ask children to watch closely as the soft soap (representing God) is dipped into the middle of the bowl. The pepper will "flee" to the outside edge of the bowl.

Share: We, like the pepper, are seasoned with sin. God, like the soap, is pure and clean. When we see God, we often tremble and flee because God is so powerful. But thanks to Jesus' death and resurrection, we have been forgiven. We can come close to God and not fear punishment. Instead, we should revere or be in awe of God's great power and love.

 Read aloud Proverbs 28:14. Then ask:
• **What does it mean to fear the Lord?** (To show Him respect; to not use His name in a wrong way; to know God is bigger than we are.)

Share: God is indeed awesome. And just when we think we understand everything about Him, He surprises us. We will someday know God when we meet Him face to face, but for now, we must fear Him and at the same time draw near to Him.

WRAP-UP

Gather everyone in a circle and have family members take turns answering this question: **What's one thing you've learned about God today?**

Next, tell kids you've got a new "Life Slogan" you'd like to share with them.

Life Slogan: Today's Life Slogan is this: "Hold God in fear and He'll draw near." Have family members repeat the slogan two or three times to help them learn it. Then encourage them to practice saying it during the week so they can talk about it at your next family night session.

Close in Prayer: Allow time for each family member to share prayer concerns and answers to prayer. Then close your time together with prayer for each concern. Thank God for listening to and caring about us.

Remember to record your prayer requests so you can refer to them in the future as you see God answering them.

⊚ How to Lead Your Child to Christ

SOME THINGS TO CONSIDER AHEAD OF TIME:

1. Realize that God is more concerned about your child's eternal destiny and happiness than you are. "The Lord is not slow in keeping His promise. . . . He is patient with you, not wanting anyone to perish, but everyone to come to repentance" (2 Peter 3:9).

2. Pray specifically beforehand that God will give you insights and wisdom in dealing with each child on his or her maturity level.

3. Don't use terms like "take Jesus into your heart," "dying and going to hell," and "accepting Christ as your personal Savior." Children are either too literal ("How does Jesus breathe in my heart?") or the words are too clichéd and trite for their understanding.

4. Deal with each child alone, and don't be in a hurry. Make sure he or she understands. Discuss. Take your time.

A FEW CAUTIONS:

1. When drawing children to Himself, Jesus said for others to "allow" them to come to Him (see Mark 10:14). Only with adults did He use the term "compel" (see Luke 14:23). Do not compel children.

2. Remember that unless the Holy Spirit is speaking to the child, there will be no genuine heart experience of regeneration. Parents, don't get caught up in the idea that Jesus will return the day before you were going to speak to your child about salvation and that it will be too late. Look at God's character—He *is* love! He is not dangling your child's soul over hell. Wait on God's timing.

   Pray with faith, believing. Be concerned, but don't push.

THE PLAN:

1. **God loves you.** Recite John 3:16 with your child's name in place of "the world."

2. **Show the child his or her need of a Savior.**

   a. Deal with sin carefully. There is one thing that cannot enter heaven—sin.

   b. Be sure your child knows what sin is. Ask him to name some (things common to children—lying, sassing, disobeying, etc.). Sin is doing or thinking anything wrong according to God's Word. It is breaking God's Law.

   c. Ask the question "Have you sinned?" If the answer is no, do not continue. Urge him to come and talk to you again when he does feel that he has sinned. Dismiss him. You may want to have prayer first, however, thanking God "for this young child who is willing to do what is right." Make it easy for him to talk to you again, but do not continue. Do not say, "Oh, yes, you have too sinned!" and then name some. With children, wait for God's conviction.

   d. If the answer is yes, continue. He may even give a personal illustration of some sin he has done recently or one that has bothered him.

   e. Tell him what God says about sin: We've all sinned ("There is no one righteous, not even one," Rom. 3:10). And because of that sin, we can't get to God ("For the wages of sin is death," Rom. 6:23). So He had to come to us ("but the gift of God is eternal life in Christ Jesus our Lord," Rom. 6:23).

   f. Relate God's gift of salvation to Christmas gifts—we don't earn them or pay for them; we just accept them and are thankful for them.

3. **Bring the child to a definite decision.**

   a. Christ must be received if salvation is to be possessed.

   b. Remember, do not force a decision.

   c. Ask the child to pray out loud in her own words. Give her some things she could say if she seems unsure. Now be prepared for a blessing! (It is best to avoid having the child repeat a memorized prayer after you. Let her think, and make it personal.)*

d. After salvation has occurred, pray for her out loud. This is a good way to pronounce a blessing on her.

4. **Lead your child into assurance.**

Show him that he will have to keep his relationship open with God through repentance and forgiveness (just like with his family or friends), but that God will always love him ("Never will I leave you; never will I forsake you," Heb. 13:5).

* If you wish to guide your child through the prayer, here is some suggested language.

"Dear God, I know that I am a sinner [have child name specific sins he or she acknowledged earlier, such as lying, stealing, disobeying, etc.]. I know that Jesus died on the cross to pay for all my sins. I ask You to forgive me of my sins. I believe that Jesus died for me and rose from the dead, and I accept Him as my Savior. Thank You for loving me. In Jesus' name. Amen."

Cumulative Topical Index

TOPIC	SCRIPTURE	WHAT YOU'LL NEED	WHERE TO FIND IT
The Acts of the Sinful Nature and the Fruit of the Spirit	Gal. 5:19-26	3x5 cards or paper, markers, and tape	IFN, p. 43
Adding Value to Money through Saving Takes Time	Matt. 6:19-21	Supplies for making cookies and a Bible	MMK, p. 89
All Have Sinned	Rom. 3:23	Raw eggs, bucket of water	BCB, p. 89
All of Our Plans Should Match God's	Ps. 139:1-18	Paper, pencils, markers, or crayons	MMK, p. 73
Avoid Things That Keep Us from Growing	Eph. 4:14-15; Heb. 5:11-14	Seeds, plants at various stages of growth or a garden or nursery to tour, Bible	CCQ, p. 77
Bad Company Corrupts Good Character	1 Cor. 15:33	Small ball, string, slips of paper, pencil, yarn or masking tape, Bible	IFN, p. 103
Be Thankful for Good Friends		Bible, art supplies, markers	IFN, p. 98
Because We Love God, We Obey His Commands		Light source, variety of objects	TC, p. 23
Being Content with What We Have	Phil. 4:11-13	Bible	CCQ, p. 17
Being Diligent Means Working Hard and Well	Gen. 39–41	Bible, paper, a pencil and other supplies depending on jobs chosen	MMK, p. 64
Being a Faithful Steward Means Managing God's Gifts Wisely	1 Peter 4:10; Luke 19:12-26	Graham crackers, peanut butter, thin stick pretzels, small marshmallows, and M & Ms®	MMK, p. 18
Being Jealous Means Wanting Things Other People Have	Gen. 37:4-5	Different size boxes of candy or other treats, and a Bible	OTS, p. 39
Being with God in Heaven Is Worth More than Anything Else	Matt. 13:44-46	Hershey's kisses candies, a Bible	NTS, p. 24
Budgeting Means Making a Plan for Using Our Money	Jud. 6–7	Table, large sheets or paper, and markers or crayons	MMK, p. 79

TOPIC	SCRIPTURE	WHAT YOU'LL NEED	WHERE TO FIND IT
Budgeting Means the Money Coming in Has to Equal the Money Going Out	Luke 14:28-35; Jud. 6–7	Supply of beans, paper, pencil, and Bible	MMK, p. 80
By Setting Aside the Time to Focus on God, We Have a Chance to Reflect on His Glory and Goodness in Our "Busy" Lives	Mark 2:27; Heb. 12:1-4	Bible, poster board, crayons and or markers, a $5 bill, tape	TC, p. 49
Change Helps Us Grow and Mature	Rom. 8:28-39	Bible	WLS, p. 39
Change Is Good	1 Kings 17:8-16	Jar or box for holding change, colored paper, tape, markers, Bible	MMK, p. 27
Christ Is Who We Serve	Col. 3:23-24	Paper, scissors, pens	IFN, p. 50
The Christmas Story Is about Jesus' Birth	Luke 2; Matt. 2	Styrofoam cones and balls of various sizes, a large box, markers or paints, tape, a Bible	NTS, p. 47
Christians Should Be Joyful Each Day	James 3:22-23; Ps. 118:24	Small plastic bottle, cork to fit bottle opening, water, vinegar, paper towel, Bible	CCQ, p. 67
Commitment and Hard Work Are Needed to Finish Strong	Gen. 6:5-22	Jigsaw puzzle, Bible	CCQ, p. 83
The Consequence of Sin Is Death	Ps. 19:1-6	Dominoes	BCB, p. 57
Contentment Is the Secret to Happiness	Matt. 6:33	Package of candies, a Bible	MMK, p. 51
Creation	Gen. 1:1; Ps. 19:1-6; Rom. 1:20	Nature book or video, Bible	IFN, p. 17
David and Bathsheba	2 Sam. 11:1–12:14	Bible	BCB, p. 90
Description of Heaven	Rev. 21:3-4, 10-27	Bible, drawing supplies	BCB, p. 76
Difficulty Can Help Us Grow	Jer. 32:17; Luke 18:27	Bible, card game like Old Maid or Crazy Eights	CCQ, p. 33
Discipline and Training Make Us Stronger	Prov. 4:23	Narrow doorway, Bible	CCQ, p. 103
Dishonesty Teaches Others to Distrust Us	Prov. 12:13	Small pebbles, eggs, a spoon, Bible	P, p. 29

TOPIC	SCRIPTURE	WHAT YOU'LL NEED	WHERE TO FIND IT
Do Not Give In to Those Around You	Matt. 14:6-12; Luke 23:13-25	Empty one two-liter plastic bottles, eye-dropper, water, a Bible	SS, p.21
Don't Be Distracted by Unimportant Things	Matt. 14:22-32	One marked penny, lots of unmarked pennies, a wrapped gift for each child, a Bible	NTS, p. 35
Don't Be Yoked with Unbelievers	2 Cor. 16:17–17:1	Milk, food coloring	IFN, p. 105
Don't Give Respect Based on Material Wealth	Eph. 6:1-8; 1 Peter 2:13-17; Ps. 119:17; James 2:1-2; 1 Tim. 4:12	Large sheet of paper, tape, a pen, Bible	IFN, p. 64
Dorcas Made Clothes and Did Good Things	Acts 9:36-42	Large pillowcases, fabric markers, scissors, a Bible	NTS, p. 71
Easter Was God's Plan for Jesus	John 3:16; Rom. 3:23; 6:23	Paper and pencils or pens, materials to make a large cross, and a Bible	HFN, p. 27
Equality Does Not Mean Contentment	Matt. 20:1-16	Money or candy bars, tape recorder or radio, Bible	WLS, p. 21
Even if We're Not in the Majority, We May Be Right	2 Tim. 3:12-17	Piece of paper, pencil, water	CCQ, p. 95
Every Day Is a Gift from God	Prov. 16:9	Bible	CCQ, p. 69
Evil Hearts Say Evil Words	Prov. 15:2-8; Luke 6:45; Eph. 4:29	Bible, small mirror	IFN, p. 79
Family Members Ought to Be Loyal to Each Other	The Book of Ruth	Shoebox, two pieces of different colored felt, seven pipe cleaners (preferably of different colors)	OTS, p. 67
Fearing God Means Being in Awe of Him and Respecting Him	Prov. 28:14	Bowl, water, pepper, soft soap, Bible	P, p. 85
Friends Sharpen One Another by Being Loyal, Unselfish, Willing to Learn, and Forgiving	Prov. 17:9, 17; 27:6, 17	Candles, matches, construction paper, permanent black marker, tape, a Bible	P, p. 71
The Fruit of the Spirit	Gal. 5:22-23; Luke 3:8; Acts 26:20	Blindfold and Bible	BCB, p. 92
God Allows Testing to Help Us Mature	James 1:2-4	Bible	BCB, p. 44
God Became a Man So We Could Understand His Love	John 14:9-10	A pet of some kind, and a Bible	HFN, p. 85

TOPIC	SCRIPTURE	WHAT YOU'LL NEED	WHERE TO FIND IT
God Can Clean Our Guilty Consciences	1 John 1:9	Small dish of bleach, dark piece of material, Bible	WLS, p. 95
God Can Do the Impossible	John 6:1-14	Bible, sturdy plank (6 or more inches wide and 6 to 8 feet long), a brick or similar object, snack of fish and crackers	CCQ, p. 31
God Can Give Us Strength		Musical instruments (or pots and pans with wooden spoons) and a snack	OTS, p. 52
God Can Guide Us Away from Satan's Traps	Ps. 119:9-11; Prov. 3:5-6	Ten or more inexpensive mousetraps, pencil, blindfold, Bible	WLS, p. 72
God Can Help Us Knock Sin Out of Our Lives	Ps. 32:1-5; 1 John 1:9	Heavy drinking glass, pie tin, small slips of paper, pencils, large raw egg, cardboard tube from a roll of toilet paper, broom, masking tape, Bible	WLS, p. 53
God Can Use Us in Unique Ways to Accomplish His Plans		Strings of cloth, clothespins or strong tape, "glow sticks" or small flashlights	OTS, p. 63
God Cares for Us Even in Hard Times	Job 1–2; 42	Bible	WLS, p. 103
God Chose to Make Dads (or Moms) as a Picture of Himself	Gen. 1:26-27	Large sheets of paper, pencils, a bright light, a picture of your family, a Bible	HFN, p. 47
God Commands Honoring for Our Benefit	Luke 15:11-32; Ex. 20:12; Deut. 5:16	Bibles	TC, p. 56
God Created the Heavens and the Earth	Gen. 1	Small tent or sheet and a rope, Christmas lights, two buckets (one with water), a coffee can with dirt, a tape recorder and cassette, and a flashlight	OTS, p. 17
God Created Us	Isa. 45:9, 64:8; Ps. 139:13	Bible and video of potter with clay	BCB, p. 43
God Created the World, Stars, Plants, Animals, and People	Gen. 1	Play dough or clay, safe shaping or cutting tools, a Bible	OTS, p. 19

Family Night
TOOL CHEST

AN INTRODUCTION TO FAMILY NIGHTS
= IFN

BASIC CHRISTIAN BELIEFS
= BCB

CHRISTIAN CHARACTER QUALITIES
= CCQ

WISDOM LIFE SKILLS
= WLS

MONEY MATTERS FOR KIDS
= MMK

HOLIDAYS FAMILY NIGHT
= HFN

BIBLE STORIES FOR PRESCHOOLERS (OLD TESTAMENT)
= OTS

SIMPLE SCIENCE
= SS

BIBLE STORIES FOR PRESCHOOLERS (NEW TESTAMENT)
= NTS

TEN COMMANDMENTS
= TC

PROVERBS
= P

TOPIC	SCRIPTURE	WHAT YOU'LL NEED	WHERE TO FIND IT
God Doesn't Like Laziness	Prov. 22:13; 6:9; 13:4; 21:25; 18:9; 12:27; 20:17; 11:18; 10:4; 14:23; 15:19; 19:15; 10:5	Microwave popcorn, microwave oven (or supplies for popping corn on the stove), Bible	P, p. 59
God Doesn't Want Us to Worry	Matt. 6:25-34; Phil. 4:6-7; Ps. 55:22	Bible, paper, pencils	CCQ, p. 39
God Forgives Those Who Confess Their Sins	1 John 1:9	Sheets of paper, tape, Bible	BCB, p. 58
God Gave Jesus a Message for Us	John 1:14,18; 8:19; 12:49-50	Goldfish in water or bug in jar, water	BCB, p. 66
God Gives and God Can Take Away	Luke 12:13-21	Bible, timer with bell or buzzer, large bowl of small candies, smaller bowl for each child	CCQ, p. 15
God Gives Us the Skills We Need to Do What He Asks of Us		Materials to make a sling (cloth, shoe-strings), plastic golf balls or marshmal-lows, stuffed animals	OTS, p. 73
God Is Greater Than We Can Understand; Yet He Reveals Himself to Us through His Word	Prov. 15:3, 8-9, 11, 25, 29;16:2, 33; 17:3, 5; 11:8, 21, 31;18:10; 21:27; 22-23; 28:29	Empty wine bottle, cork, cloth napkin, Bible	P, p. 83
God Is Holy	Ex. 3:1-6	Masking tape, baby powder or corn starch, broom, Bible	IFN, p. 31
God Is Invisible, Powerful, and Real	John 1:18, 4:24; Luke 24:36-39	Balloons, balls, refrigerator magnets, Bible	IFN, p. 15
God Is the Source of Our Strength	Jud. 16	Oversized sweat-shirt, balloons, mop heads or other items to use as wigs, items to stack to make pillars, a Bible	OTS, p. 61
God Is Our Only Source of Strength	Isa. 40:29-31	Straws, fresh baking potatoes, a Bible	SS, p.33
God Is with Us	Ex. 25:10-22; Deut. 10:1-5; Josh. 3:14-17; 1 Sam. 3:3; 2 Sam. 6:12-15	A large cardboard box, two broom han-dles, a utility knife, strong tape, gold spray paint, and a Bible	OTS, p. 49
God Keeps His Promises	Gen. 6–9:16	Plastic coffee can lid, flashlight, bubble solution, straw, a Bible	SS, p.75

TOPIC	SCRIPTURE	WHAT YOU'LL NEED	WHERE TO FIND IT
God Keeps His Promises	Gen. 9:13, 15	Sheets of colored cellophane, cardboard, scissors, tape, a Bible, a lamp or large flashlight	OTS, p. 25
God Knew His Plans for Us	Jer. 29:11	Two puzzles and a Bible	BCB, p. 19
God Knew Moses Would Be Found by Pharaoh's Daughter	Ex. 2:1-10	A doll or stuffed animal, a basket, and a blanket	OTS, p. 43
God Knows All about Us	Ps. 139:2-4; Matt. 10:30	3x5 cards, a pen	BCB, p. 17
God Knows Everything	Isa. 40:13-14; Eph. 4:1-6	Bible	IFN, p. 15
God Knows the Plan for Our Lives	Rom. 8:28	Three different 25–50 piece jigsaw puzzles, Bible	WLS, p. 101
God Looks at the Heart	1 Sam. 16:7; Gal. 2:6	4 cans of pop (2 regular and 2 diet), 1 large tub, duct tape, water, a Bible	SS, p. 81
God Looks beyond the Mask and into Our Hearts		Costumes	HFN, p. 65
God Loves It When We Use the Gifts He's Given Us to Help Others	Prov. 11:24; 14:21	Box of tools, Bible	P, p. 72
God Loves and Protects Us	Matt. 6:26-27	One or two raw eggs, a sink or bucket, a Bible	SS, p. 15
God Loves Us So Much, He Sent Jesus	John 3:16; Eph. 2:8-9	I.O.U. for each family member	IFN, p. 34
God Made Our Family Unique by Placing Each of Us in It		Different color paint for each family member, toothpicks or paintbrushes to dip into paint, white paper, Bible	BCB, p. 110
God Made Us		Building blocks, such as Tinkertoys, Legos, or K'nex	HFN, p. 15
God Made Us in His Image	Gen. 1:24-27	Play dough or clay and Bible	BCB, p. 24
God Never Changes	Ecc. 3:1-8; Heb. 13:8	Paper, pencils, Bible	WLS, p. 37
God Owns Everything; He Gives Us Things to Manage		Large sheet of poster board or newsprint and colored markers	MMK, p. 17
God Points Us toward His Plan	Prov. 13:13; 24:10; 27:21; 22:17-19; 29:25	Construction paper, tape, glue, Bible	P, p. 54

TOPIC	SCRIPTURE	WHAT YOU'LL NEED	WHERE TO FIND IT
God Provides a Way Out of Temptation	1 Cor. 10:12-13; James 1:13-14; 4:7; 1 John 2:15-17	Bible	IFN, p. 88
God Sees Who We Really Are—We Can Never Fool Him	1 Sam. 16:7	Construction paper, scissors, crayons or markers, a hat or bowl, and a Bible	HFN, p. 66
God Strengthens Us and Protects Us from Satan	2 Thes. 3:3; Ps. 18:2-3	Two un-inflated black balloons, water, a candle, matches, a Bible	SS, p. 16
God Teaches Us about Love through Others	1 Cor. 13	Colored paper, markers, crayons, scissors, tape or glue, and a Bible	HFN, p. 22
God Used Plagues to Tell Pharaoh to Let Moses and His People Go	Ex. 7–12	A clear glass, red food coloring, water, and a Bible	OTS, p. 44
God Uses Many Ways to Get Our Attention	Dan. 5	Large sheets of paper or poster board, tape, finger-paint, and a Bible	OTS, p. 79
God Wants Our Best Effort in All We Do	Col. 3:23-24	Children's blocks or a large supply of cardboard boxes	MMK, p. 63
God Wants a Passionate Relationship with Us	Rev. 3:16	Pans of hot, cold, and lukewarm water, hot and cold drinks	SS, p. 69
God Wants Us to Be Diligent in Our Work	Prov. 6:6-11; 1 Thes. 4:11-12	Video about ants or picture books or encyclopedia, Bible	CCQ, p. 55
God Wants Us to Be Moldable	Prov. 29:1	Flour, alum, salad oil, salt, boiling water, a Bible	P, p. 67
God Wants Us to Get Closer to Him	James 4:8; 1 John 4:7-12	Hidden Bibles, clues to find them	BCB, p. 33
God Wants Us to Give to Others in Love		Candy	NTS, p. 54
God Wants Us to Glorify Him	Ps. 24:1; Luke 12:13-21	Paper, pencils, Bible	WLS, p. 47
God Wants Us to Reflect His Word	James 1:19-25	Bible, hand mirror, cardboard, a flashlight	NTS, p. 84
God Wants Us to Work and Be Helpful	2 Thes. 3:6-15	Several undone chores, Bible	CCQ, p. 53
God Will Never Leave Us or Forsake Us	Matt. 28:20	Long sheet of paper, pencil, scissors, tape or glue, a Bible	SS, p. 76
God Will Send the Holy Spirit	John 14:23-26; 1 Cor. 2:12	Flashlights, small treats, Bible	IFN, p. 39

TOPIC	SCRIPTURE	WHAT YOU'LL NEED	WHERE TO FIND IT
God Will Separate Those Who Believe in Jesus from Those Who Don't	Matt. 13:47-49; John 3:16	Large box, crayons or markers, a large bath towel, candy-size rocks, candy, wax paper, a Bible	NTS, p. 29
God Will Separate Those Who Love Him from Those Who Don't	Matt. 25:31-46	Coarse salt, ground pepper, plastic spoon, wool cloth, a Bible	SS, p. 64
God's Covenant with Noah	Gen. 8:13-21; 9:8-17	Bible, paper, crayons or markers	BCB, p. 52
God's Name Represents His Character, Person-age, Nature, Reputa-tion, and Role	Ex. 20:7; Matt. 5:34	Dictionary, paper, pencils, a Bible	TC, p. 41
A Good Friend Encourages Us to Do What Jesus Would Do	Ecc. 4:9-12	Strips of cardboard, books, 50 pennies, a Bible	SS, p. 82
Guarding the Gate to Our Minds	Prov. 4:13; 2 Cor. 11:3; Phil. 4:8	Bible, poster board for each family member, old maga-zines, glue, scissors, markers	CCQ, p. 23
The Holy Spirit Helps Us	Eph. 1:17; John 14:15-17; Acts 1:1-11; Eph. 3:16-17; Rom. 8:26-27; 1 Cor. 2:11-16	Bible	BCB, p. 99
The Holy Spirit Helps Us to Be a Light in the Dark World	Matt. 5:14-16; 1 Tim. 2:1-4	Wintergreen or Cryst-O-Mint Lifesavers, a Bible	SS, p. 40
Honesty Means Being Sure We Tell the Truth and Are Fair	Prov. 10:9; 11:3; 12:5; 14:2; 28:13	A bunch of coins and a Bible	MMK, p. 58
Honor the Holy Spirit, Don't Block Him	1 John 4:4; 1 Cor. 6:19-20	Bible, blow-dryer or vacuum cleaner with exit hose, a Ping-Pong ball	CCQ, p. 47
Honor Your Parents	Ex. 20:12	Paper, pencil, treats, umbrella, soft objects, masking tape, pen, Bible	IFN, p. 55
Honoring Your Parents Teaches You to Honor God		Balloon, two differ-ent pieces of colored paper, pencils	TC, p. 55
How Big Is an Ark?		Large open area, buckets of water, cans of animal food, bags of dog food, and four flags	OTS, p. 24

Family Night
TOOL CHEST

AN INTRODUCTION TO FAMILY NIGHTS
= IFN

BASIC CHRISTIAN BELIEFS
= BCB

CHRISTIAN CHARACTER QUALITIES
= CCQ

WISDOM LIFE SKILLS
= WLS

MONEY MATTERS FOR KIDS
= MMK

HOLIDAYS FAMILY NIGHT
= HFN

BIBLE STORIES FOR PRESCHOOLERS (OLD TESTAMENT)
= OTS

SIMPLE SCIENCE
= SS

BIBLE STORIES FOR PRESCHOOLERS (NEW TESTAMENT)
= NTS

TEN COMMANDMENTS
= TC

PROVERBS
= P

TOPIC	SCRIPTURE	WHAT YOU'LL NEED	WHERE TO FIND IT
A Humble Heart Pleases God	Prov. 15:33; 16:5, 18; 29:23	Handout of cutout, a Bible	P, p. 33
Idols Come in All Shapes and Sizes	Isa. 46:1-11; Col. 3:5-6	A favorite thing from each child	TC, p. 37
If We Accept Jesus as Savior, We'll Get into Heaven	Rev. 20:15, 21:27	Bible, marshmallows, cotton candy, ice cream	NTS, p. 90
If We Confess Our Sins, Jesus Will Forgive Us	Heb. 12:1;1 John 1:9	Magic slate, candies, paper, pencils, bathrobe ties or soft rope, items to weigh someone down, and a Bible	HFN, p. 28
The Importance of Your Name Being Written in the Book of Life	Rev. 20:11-15; 21:27	Bible, phone book, access to other books with family name	BCB, p. 74
Intent to Commit Sexual Sin Is as Wrong as the Act Itself	Matt. 5:27-28; Ps. 119:9	Three large boxes and a Bible	TC, p. 69
Investing and Saving Adds Value to Money	Prov. 21:20	Two and a half dollars for each family member	MMK, p. 87
It Is Important to Spend Time Praising God	Ps. 66:1; 81:1; 95:1; 98:4; 100:1	Plastic straws, scissors, a Bible	SS, p. 52
It's Better to Follow the Truth	Rom. 1:25; Prov. 2:1-5	Second set of clues, box of candy or treats, Bible	WLS, p. 86
It's Better to Wait for Something Than to Borrow Money to Buy It	2 Kings 4:1-7; Prov. 22:7	Magazines, advertisements, paper, a pencil, Bible	MMK, p. 103
It's Difficult to Be a Giver When You're a Debtor		Pennies or other coins	MMK, p. 105
It's Easy to Follow a Lie, but It Leads to Disappointment		Clues as described in lesson, empty box	WLS, p. 85
It Is a Good Thing to Say Encouraging Words	Prov. 16:24; 27:6; 13:14; 18:21	Colorfully decorated boxes, stickers, paper, pens or pencils, Bible	P, p. 48
It's Important to Listen to Jesus' Message		Bible	BCB, p. 68
It's Not Always Easy to Do What Jesus Wants Us to Do	Matt. 7:13	Toy blocks, a narrow board, two cinder blocks, a Bible	NTS, p. 17
It's Not Easy to Break a Pattern of Sin	James 1:12-15	Paper, pan, water, a Bible	SS, p. 63

TOPIC	SCRIPTURE	WHAT YOU'LL NEED	WHERE TO FIND IT
It Takes Self-discipline to Fight Temptation	Prov. 6:20-24; 7:1-5	Crayons or markers, paper, Bibles	P, p. 23
It Takes Work to Have a Teachable Heart	Prov. 25:12; 12:15, 15:31; 13:18	"Medal" for each family member, Bible	P, p. 65
Jesus Came to Die for Our Sins	Rom. 5:8	A large piece of cardboard, markers, scissors, tape, and a Bible	HFN, p. 91
Jesus Came to Give Us Eternal Life	Mark 16:12-14	A calculator, a calendar, a sheet of paper, and a pencil	HFN, p. 91
Jesus Came to Teach Us about God	John 1:14, 18	Winter clothing, bread crumbs, a Bible	HFN, p. 92
Jesus Came to Show Us How Much God Loves Us	John 3:16	Supplies to make an Advent wreath, and a Bible	HFN, p. 89
Jesus Comes to Find Us When We Are Lost	Luke 15:1-7	Bible, blindfolds	NTS, p. 61
Jesus Cried Just Like We Do	John 11	Children's Bible storybook, a Bible, or video, *The Easter Promise*	NTS, p. 65
Jesus Died for Our Sins	Luke 22:1-6; Mark 14:12-26; Luke 22:47-54; Luke 22:55-62; Matt. 27:1-10; Matt. 27:11-31; Luke 23:26-34	Seven plastic eggs, slips of paper with Scripture verses, and a Bible	HFN, p. 33
Jesus Dies on the Cross	John 14:6	6-foot 2x4, 3-foot 2x4, hammers, nails, Bible	IFN, p. 33
Jesus Has Power over Death		Toilet paper rolls	NTS, p. 66
Jesus Promises Us New Bodies and a New Home in Heaven	Phil. 3:20-21; Luke 24:36-43; Rev. 21:1-4	Ingredients for making pumpkin pie, and a Bible	HFN, p. 61
Jesus Took Our Sins to the Cross and Freed Us from Being Bound Up in Sin	Rom. 6:23; 5:8; 6:18	Soft rope or heavy yarn, a watch with a second hand, thread, and a Bible	HFN, p. 53
Jesus Took the Punishment We Deserve	Rom. 6:23; John 3:16; Rom. 5:8-9	Bathrobe, list of bad deeds	IFN, p. 26
Jesus Wants Us to Do the Right Thing			NTS, p. 18

TOPIC	SCRIPTURE	WHAT YOU'LL NEED	WHERE TO FIND IT
Jesus Was Victorious Over Death and Sin	Luke 23:35-43; Luke 23:44-53; Matt. 27:59-61; Luke 23:54–24:12	Five plastic eggs—four with Scripture verses, and a Bible	HFN, p. 36
Jesus Washes His Followers' Feet	John 13:1-17	Bucket of warm soapy water, towels, Bible	IFN, p. 63
Joshua and the Battle of Jericho	Josh. 1:16-18; 6:1-21	Paper, pencil, dots on paper that, when connected, form a star	IFN, p. 57
Knowing God's Word Helps Us Know What Stand to Take	2 Tim. 3:1-5	Current newspaper, Bible	CCQ, p. 93
Look to God, Not Others	Phil. 4:11-13	Magazines or newspapers, a chair, several pads of small yellow stickies, Bible	WLS, p. 24
Love Is Unselfish	1 Cor. 13	A snack and a Bible	HFN, p. 21
Love Means Putting Others' Needs above Our Own	Luke 10:25-37	Children's Bible storybook, two equal-length strips of wood, paper, marker, costumes, a Bible	NTS, p. 53
Loving Money Is Wrong	1 Tim. 6:6-10	Several rolls of coins, masking tape, Bible	WLS, p. 45
Lying Can Hurt People	Acts 5:1-11	Two pizza boxes—one empty and one with a fresh pizza—and a Bible	MMK, p. 57
Lying Has Consequences	Ex. 20:16; Matt. 5:37	Baseball bat or stick of same length, masking tape, Bible	TC, p. 81
Meeting Goals Requires Planning	Prov. 3:5-6	Paper, scissors, pencils, a treat, a Bible	MMK, p. 71
Moms Are Special and Important to Us and to God	Prov. 24:3-4	Confetti, streamers, a comfortable chair, a wash basin with warm water, two cloths, and a Bible	HFN, p. 41
Moms Model Jesus' Love When They Serve Gladly	2 Tim. 1:4-7	Various objects depending on chosen activity and a Bible	HFN, p. 42
Money and Worldly Accomplishments Don't Make Us Successful in God's Eyes	Prov. 12:3; 25:27; 27:2	Sturdy board or table leaf, blindfold, Bible	P, p. 77
The More We Know God, the More We Know His Voice	John 10:1-6	Bible	BCB, p. 35

TOPIC	SCRIPTURE	WHAT YOU'LL NEED	WHERE TO FIND IT
Murders, and the Attitude that Causes People to Murder, Is Sinful	Ex. 20:13; Matt. 22:37-39; Gen. 4:8-10	Pennies and a Bible	TC, p. 61
Nicodemus Asks Jesus about Being Born Again	John 3:7, 50-51; 19:39-40	Bible, paper, pencil, costume	BCB, p. 81
Noah Obeyed God When He Built the Ark	Gen. 6:14-16	A large refrigerator box, markers or paints, self-adhesive paper, stuffed animals, a Bible, utility knife	OTS, p. 23
Nothing Is Impossible When It Is in God's Will	Matt. 21:28	Hard-boiled egg, butter, glass bottle, paper, matches, a Bible	SS, p. 34
Obedience Has Good Rewards		Planned outing everyone will enjoy, directions on 3x5 cards, number cards	IFN, p. 59
Obey God First		Paper, markers, scissors, and blindfolds	OTS, p. 80
Only a Relationship with God Can Fill Our Need	Isa. 55:1-2	Doll that requires batteries, batteries for the doll, dollar bill, pictures of a house, an expensive car, and a pretty woman or handsome man, Bible	WLS, p. 62
Only God Can Provide for Our Needs	Ex. 20:4-6	Items representing children's favorite media stars and a Bible	TC, p. 35
Our Actions Should Mirror God, Not the World	Rom. 12:2	Regular glass, dried peas, a wine glass, a pie tin, water, a Bible	SS, p. 57
Our Conscience Helps Us Know Right from Wrong	Rom. 2:14-15	Foods with a strong smell, blindfold, Bible	WLS, p. 93
Our Minds Should Be Filled with Good, Not Evil	Phil 4:8; Ps. 119:9, 11	Bible, bucket of water, several large rocks	CCQ, p. 26
Our Tongue Is Powerful and Should Be Used to Glorify God	James 3:5-8	Squirt gun, pie pan, Pop Rocks candy, a Bible	SS, p. 51
Parable of the Talents	Matt. 25:14-30	Bible	IFN, p. 73
Parable of the Vine and Branches	John 15:1-8	Tree branch, paper, pencils, Bible	IFN, p. 95

Family Night
TOOL CHEST

AN INTRODUCTION TO FAMILY NIGHTS
= IFN

BASIC CHRISTIAN BELIEFS
= BCB

CHRISTIAN CHARACTER QUALITIES
= CCQ

WISDOM LIFE SKILLS
= WLS

MONEY MATTERS FOR KIDS
= MMK

HOLIDAYS FAMILY NIGHT
= HFN

BIBLE STORIES FOR PRESCHOOLERS (OLD TESTAMENT)
= OTS

SIMPLE SCIENCE
= SS

BIBLE STORIES FOR PRESCHOOLERS (NEW TESTAMENT)
= NTS

TEN COMMANDMENTS
= TC

PROVERBS
= P

TOPIC	SCRIPTURE	WHAT YOU'LL NEED	WHERE TO FIND IT
People Came to See Jesus and Bring Him Gifts	Luke 2; Matt. 2	Styrofoam cones and balls of various sizes, a large box, markers or paints, tape, a Bible	NTS, p. 48
People, Like Plants, Need Good Soil to Grow	Mark 4:3-8, 13-20	Cake pan, aluminum foil, small stones, seeds, toothpicks, potting soil, a Bible	NTS, p. 41
People Look at Outside Appearance, but God Looks at the Heart	1 Sam. 17	Slings from activity on p. 73, plastic golf balls or marshmallows, a tape measure, cardboard, markers, and a Bible	OTS, p. 75
People Who Have the Gift of Hospitality Open Their Homes and Serve Others		Snacks and supplies for a nice meal	NTS, p. 78
Persecution Brings a Reward		Bucket, bag of ice, marker, one-dollar bill	WLS, p. 32
Planning Helps Us Finish Strong	Phil. 3:10-14	Flight map on p. 86, paper, pencils, Bible	CCQ, p. 85
Pray, Endure, and Be Glad When We're Persecuted	Matt. 5:11-12, 44; Rom. 12:14; 1 Cor. 4:12	Notes, Bible, candle or flashlight, dark small space	WLS, p. 29
Prayer Keeps Us Connected to God	Prov. 15:29	Wooden 6- to 12-inch dowel 1/4" in diameter, paper, tape, Bible	P, p. 53
Priscilla Had the Gift of Hospitality	Acts 18:1-4; 18-26; Rom. 16:3-5	Large sheet, rope, clothespins, a Bible	NTS, p. 77
Proverbs Teaches Us How to Live Godly Lives	Prov. 1:1-7	Ingredients for baking a cake, Bible	P, p.15
Putting God First Builds a Solid Relationship	Mark 6:35; Luke 4:16; Mark 13:31; Luke 12:31	Wide-mouth glass jar, large rocks, sand, water, permanent marker, a Bible	SS, p. 70
Remember All God Has Done for You	Ex. 25:1; 16:34; Num. 17:10; Deut. 31:26	Ark of the covenant from p. 49, cardboard or Styrofoam, crackers, a stick, and a Bible	OTS, p. 51
Remember What God Has Done for You	Gen. 12:7-8; 13:18; 22:9	Bricks or large rocks, paint, and a Bible	OTS, p. 31
The Responsibilities of Families	Eph. 5:22-33; 6:1-4	Photo albums, Bible	BCB, p. 101
The Road of the Foolish Is Hard; the Road of the Wise Has Rewards	Prov. 10:21; 14:15-16; 15:14; 16:16, 22; 17:10; 19:25; 29:8, 11	Paper cups, a 4-foot-long 2x4, a food prize, Bible	P, p. 41

TOPIC	SCRIPTURE	WHAT YOU'LL NEED	WHERE TO FIND IT
Satan Looks for Ways to Trap Us	Luke 4:1-13	Cardboard box, string, stick, small ball, Bible	WLS, p. 69
Self-control Helps Us Resist the Enemy	1 Peter 5:8-9; 1 Peter 2:11-12	Blindfold, watch or timer, feather or other "tickly" item, Bible	CCQ, p. 101
Serve One Another in Love	Gal. 5:13	Bag of small candies, at least three per child	IFN, p. 47
Sex Was Given to Adults as a Gift to Be Enjoyed Only in Marriage, as a True Sign of Commitment and Trust	1 Thes. 4:3-8; Ex. 20:4-6	Child's favorite wrapped candy, masking tape, a Bible	TC, p. 67
Share God's Love with Others So They Can Join Us in Heaven		Rocks, plastic bags, paper, pencils	NTS, p. 30
Sin and Busyness Interfere with Our Prayers	Luke 10:38-42; Ps. 46:10; Matt. 5:23-24; 1 Peter 3:7	Bible, two paper cups, two paper clips, long length of fishing line	CCQ, p. 61
Sin Separates Humanity	Gen. 3:1-24	Bible, clay creations, piece of hardened clay or play dough	BCB, p. 25
Some Places Aren't Open to Everyone		Book or magazine with "knock-knock" jokes	BCB, p. 73
Some Things in Life Are Out of Our Control		Blindfolds	BCB, p. 41
Sometimes God Surprises Us with Great Things	Gen. 15:15	Large sheet of poster board, straight pins or straightened paper clips, a flashlight, and a Bible	OTS, p. 32
Sometimes We Face Things That Seem Impossible		Bunch of cardboard boxes or blocks	OTS, p. 55
Sour Words Can Hurt Other People	Prov. 6:16-19; 15:4	Lemon slices, glasses of water, Bible	P, p. 47
Stand Strong in the Lord	Prov. 1:8-10; 12:3	A jar, string, chair, fan, small weight, a Bible	SS, p. 22
Temptation Takes Our Eyes Off God		Fishing pole, items to catch, timer, Bible	IFN, p. 85
The Ten Commandments Are the Standards for How God Wants Us to Live		Target with 10 holes, balls, bean bags or rolled socks	TC, p. 15

AN INTRODUCTION TO FAMILY NIGHTS
= IFN

BASIC CHRISTIAN BELIEFS
= BCB

CHRISTIAN CHARACTER QUALITIES
= CCQ

WISDOM LIFE SKILLS
= WLS

MONEY MATTERS FOR KIDS
= MMK

HOLIDAYS FAMILY NIGHT
= HFN

BIBLE STORIES FOR PRESCHOOLERS (OLD TESTAMENT)
= OTS

SIMPLE SCIENCE
= SS

BIBLE STORIES FOR PRESCHOOLERS (NEW TESTAMENT)
= NTS

TEN COMMANDMENTS
= TC

PROVERBS
= P

TOPIC	SCRIPTURE	WHAT YOU'LL NEED	WHERE TO FIND IT
The Ten Commandments Help Us to Identify What Sin Is in Today's World	Ex. 20	Paper, pens or pencils, and a Bible	TC, p. 21
The Ten Commandments Show Us Our Sinfulness and Our Need for a Savior	Rom. 3:20; 7:7-20	Butcher paper, pens, measuring tape, and a Bible	TC, p. 17
Test What the World Offers for Consistency with Jesus' Teachings	1 John 4:1	Candle, apple, almond, a Bible	SS, p. 58
There Are Only Two Things That Will Last, People (Relationships) and God's Word	Matt. 6:33	Paper, markers, a Bible	TC, p. 87
There Is a Difference between Needs and Wants	Prov. 31:16; Matt. 6:21	Paper, pencils, glasses of drinking water, a soft drink	MMK, p. 95
There Is Only One True God We Can Trust and Believe In	Ex. 20:3	Small cups that look identical, a small object (such as a ball), a Bible	TC, p. 27
Things That Are Important to Us Don't Always Cost a Lot of Money		Stuffed toy, candy bar, toys, etc.	NTS, p. 23
Those Who Don't Believe Are Foolish	Ps. 44:1	Ten small pieces of paper, pencil, Bible	IFN, p. 19
A Time of Rest Helps Us to Refocus on God and Brings Purpose to All Our Weekly Activity— to Serve Him	Gen. 2:2-3; Ex. 20:8-11; 31:12-17	Bible, balloons, markers, 1 small stone per child, paper, and pencils	TC, p. 47
Tithing Means Giving One-Tenth Back to God	Gen. 28:10-22; Ps. 3:9-10	All family members need ten similar items each, a Bible	MMK, p. 33
To Get to Heaven, Your Name Must Be in the Book of Life		Phone book, paper, crayons or markers	NTS, p. 89
The Tongue Is Small but Powerful	James 3:3-12	Video, news magazine or picture book showing devastation of fire, match, candle, Bible	IFN, p. 77
The Treasure of a Thankful Heart Is Contentment	Eph. 5:20	3x5 cards, pencils, fun prizes, and a Bible	HFN, p. 72
Trials Help Us Grow	James 1:2-4	Sugar cookie dough, cookie cutters, baking sheets, miscellaneous baking supplies, Bible	WLS, p. 15

TOPIC	SCRIPTURE	WHAT YOU'LL NEED	WHERE TO FIND IT
Trials Test How We've Grown	James 1:12	Bible	WLS, p. 17
Trust Is Important	Matt. 6:25-34	Each person needs an item he or she greatly values	MMK, p. 25
The Truth Is a Delight to God	Prov. 6:16-19; 11:1; Ex.20:16; Prov.12:19	Small candies, rubber bands, large serving spoons, a cloth napkin, a marker, Bible	P, p. 27
Truth Is the Opposite of Lying, and God Is Truth	Matt. 12:36-37	Two magnets, a Bible	TC, p. 83
We All Have Weaknesses and Will Be Attacked by Satan	1 Kings 11:3-4; 2 Cor. 12:9-10	Two pieces of plain white paper, a pencil, a Bible	SS, p. 28
We All Sin	Rom. 3:23	Target and items to throw	IFN, p. 23
We Are a Family for Life, Forever	Ruth 1:4	Shoebox; scissors; paper or cloth; magnets; photos of family members, friends, others; and a Bible	OTS, p. 68
We Are Made in God's Image	Gen. 2:7; Ps. 139:13-16	Paper bags, candies, a Bible, supplies for making gingerbread cookies	HFN, p. 17
We Are Successful in God's Eyes When We Are Faithful to Obey His Instruction	Prov. 28:12; 13:5; 22:4; 19:8	Cotton balls, spoons, bowl or glass, Bible	P, p. 79
We Become a New Creation When Jesus Comes into Our Hearts	Matt. 23:25-28; Rev. 3:20; 2 Cor. 5:17; Eph. 2:10; 2 Cor. 4:7-10; Matt. 5:14-16; 2 Cor. 4:6	Pumpkin, newspaper, sharp knife, a spoon, a candle, matches, and a Bible	HFN, p. 59
We Can Communicate with Each Other			BCB, p. 65
We Can Do Good Things for Others	1 Cor. 13:4	Newsprint or a large sheet of paper, markers or crayons, children's clothing, money to buy new clothes, a Bible	NTS, p. 72
We Can Fight the Temptation to Want More Stuff	Matt. 4:1-11; Heb. 13:5	Television, paper, a pencil, Bible	MMK, p. 49
We Can Give Joyfully to Others	Luke 10:25-37	Bible, soft yarn	MMK, p. 41

TOPIC	SCRIPTURE	WHAT YOU'LL NEED	WHERE TO FIND IT
We Can Help Each Other	Prov. 27:17	Masking tape, bowl of unwrapped candies, rulers, yardsticks, or dowel rods	BCB, p. 110
We Can Help People When We Give Generously	2 Cor. 6–7	Variety of supplies, depending on chosen activity	MMK, p. 43
We Can Learn about God from Mom (or Dad)		Supplies to make a collage (magazines, paper, tape or glue, scissors)	HFN, p. 49
We Can Learn and Grow from Good and Bad Situations	Gen. 37–48; Rom. 8:29	A Bible and a camera (optional)	OTS, p. 37
We Can Love by Helping Those in Need	Heb. 13:1-3		IFN, p. 48
We Can Show Love through Respecting Family Members		Paper and pen	IFN, p. 66
We Can't Hide from God		Supplies will vary	OTS, p. 85
We Can't Take Back the Damage of Our Words		Tube of toothpaste for each child, $10 bill	IFN, p. 78
We Deserve Punishment for Our Sins	Rom. 6:23	Dessert, other materials as decided	IFN, p. 24
We Give to God because We're Thankful		Supplies for a celebration dinner, also money for each family member	MMK, p. 36
We Have All We Need in Our Lives	Ecc. 3:11	Paper, pencils, Bible	WLS, p. 61
We Have a New Life in Christ	John 3:3; 2 Cor. 5:17	Video or picture book of caterpillar forming a cocoon then a butterfly, or a tadpole becoming a frog, or a seed becoming a plant	BCB, p. 93
We Have Much to Be Thankful For	1 Chron. 16:4-36	Unpopped popcorn, a bowl, supplies for popping popcorn, and a Bible	HFN, p. 79
We Know Others by Our Relationships with Them		Copies of questionnaire, pencils, Bible	BCB, p. 31
We Must Be in Constant Contact with God		Blindfold	CCQ, p. 63
We Must Choose to Obey		3x5 cards or slips of paper, markers, and tape	IFN, p. 43

TOPIC	SCRIPTURE	WHAT YOU'LL NEED	WHERE TO FIND IT
We Must Either Choose Christ or Reject Christ	Matt. 12:30	Clear glass jar, cooking oil, water, spoon, Bible	CCQ, p. 96
We Must Give Thanks in All Circumstances	1 Thes. 5:18	A typical family meal, cloth strips, and a Bible	HFN, p. 77
We Must Guard Our Minds against Temptation	Prov. 5:1-2, 7-8, 21-23	Golf balls, blanket, empty coffee cans, Bible	P, p. 21
We Must Hold Firm to Our Faith and Depend on God for Strength	Eph. 6:16	Balloons, long darts or shish kebab skewers, cooking oil, a Bible	SS, p. 27
We Must Learn How Much Responsibility We Can Handle		Building blocks, watch with second hand, paper, pencil	IFN, p. 71
We Must Listen	Prov. 1:5; 8-9; 4:1	Bible, other supplies for the task you choose	WLS, p. 77
We Must "Root" Ourselves in Jesus and Live by God's Word	Mark 4:1-24	A potted plant, light-weight cardboard, crayons, scissors, a Bible	NTS, p. 42
We Must Stay Focused on Jesus So We Don't Fall		Masking tape	NTS, p. 36
We Must Think Before We Speak	James 1:19	Bible	WLS, p. 79
We Must Work Hard to Become Wise One Step at a Time	Prov. 1:3-7; 19:25; 12:11; 29:11; 10:13; 15:21	Big box, lots of heavy books, Bible	P, p. 43
We Must Work Hard to Learn from the Proverbs and Gain Wisdom	Prov. 1:7	Toothpicks, Bible	P, p. 16
We Need to Feed on God's Word to Grow in Christ	Ps. 119:105; 2 Chron. 34:31; Acts 17:11; James 1:22-25	Raisins, clear drinking glass, a two-liter bottle of clear soft drink, a Bible	SS, p. 46
We Need to Grow Closer to Jesus Each Day	Acts 9:1-18	Pitcher, lemonade mix (sugarless), sugar, dry ice, a Bible	SS, p. 45
We Need to Grow Physically, Emotionally, and Spiritually	1 Peter 2:2	Photograph albums or videos of your children at different ages, tape measure, bathroom scale, Bible	CCQ, p. 75
We Need to Respect Each Other's Property	Ex. 20:15	Valuable family items	TC, p. 75

Family Night
TOOL CHEST

AN INTRODUCTION TO FAMILY NIGHTS
= IFN

BASIC CHRISTIAN BELIEFS
= BCB

CHRISTIAN CHARACTER QUALITIES
= CCQ

WISDOM LIFE SKILLS
= WLS

MONEY MATTERS FOR KIDS
= MMK

HOLIDAYS FAMILY NIGHT
= HFN

BIBLE STORIES FOR PRESCHOOLERS (OLD TESTAMENT)
= OTS

SIMPLE SCIENCE
= SS

BIBLE STORIES FOR PRESCHOOLERS (NEW TESTAMENT)
= NTS

TEN COMMANDMENTS
= TC

PROVERBS
= P

TOPIC	SCRIPTURE	WHAT YOU'LL NEED	WHERE TO FIND IT
We Need to Treat His Name With Respect for It Represents God Who Is Holy	Ps. 99:3	Eggs, checkbook, a Bible	TC, p. 43
We Need to Try to Solve Our Differences and Forgive Before Our Attitude or Actions Become Wrongful	Matt. 5:23-26; 6:9-13	Basketballs, a bowl of M&Ms®, and a Bible	TC, p. 63
We Prove Who We Are When What We Do Reflects What We Say	James 1:22; 2:14-27	A bag of candy, a rope, and a Bible	HFN, p. 67
We Reap What We Sow	Gal. 6:7	Candy bar, Bible	IFN, p. 55
We Should Be on Guard Against "Wanting" for True Happiness Is Not Found in Things		Pennies or candy and a box	TC, p. 88
We Should Do What God Wants Even If We Don't Think We Can		A powerful fan, large sheet of light-weight black plastic, duct tape, and a flashlight	OTS, p. 86
We Should Live God-Centered Lives	Matt. 4:10	24 dominoes or small blocks for each family member, a Bible	TC, p. 29
We Should Stamp Out Pride in Our Lives	Prov. 11:2; 13:10; 16:19; 18:12	3x5 cards, markers, Bible	P, p. 36
We Shouldn't Value Possessions Over Everything Else	1 Tim. 6:7-8	Box is optional	CCQ, p. 18
When a Sheep Is Lost, the Shepherd Finds It		Shoe box, felt, pom pom balls	NTS, p. 58
When God Sent Jesus to Earth, God Chose Me	Luke 1:26-38; John 3:16; Matt. 14:23	Going to choose a Christmas tree or other special decoration, a Bible, and hot chocolate	HFN, p. 83
When We Accept Jesus' Gift of Salvation, We Receive the Holy Spirit	John 3:5-8	1/4-full roll of toilet paper, a blow dryer, a dowel rod, a Bible	SS, p. 39
When We Focus on What We Don't Have, We Get Unhappy	1 Tim. 6:9-10; 1 Thes. 5:18; Phil. 4:11-13	A glass, water, paper, crayons, and a Bible	HFN, p. 71

TOPIC	SCRIPTURE	WHAT YOU'LL NEED	WHERE TO FIND IT
When We See Something Wrong with the Way We Act We Should Fix It	James 1:22-24	Clothing, a large mirror, a Bible	NTS, p. 83
When We're Set Free from Sin, We Have the Freedom to Choose, and the Responsibility to Serve	Gal. 5:13-15	Candies, soft rope, and a Bible	HFN, p. 55
Wise Spending Means Getting Good Value for What We Buy	Luke 15:11-32	Money and a Bible	MMK, p. 97
With Help, Life Is a Lot Easier		Supplies to do the chore you choose	BCB, p. 101
Wolves in Sheeps' Clothing	Matt. 7:15-20	Ten paper sacks, a marker, ten small items, Bible	IFN, p. 97
Work as Unto the Lord	Prov. 28:19; 22:29; 12:14; 13:4; 6:6-8; Col. 3:23	Pinata (or supplies to make one), broomstick, Bible	P, p. 60
Worrying Doesn't Change Anything		Board, inexpensive doorbell buzzer, a 9-volt battery, extra length of electrical wire, a large belt, assorted tools	CCQ, p. 37
You Can Choose to Obey or Not Obey, but You Can't Choose the Consequences	Josh. 6:12-17; 7:1-26	Bandana and a Bible	TC, p. 76
You Look Like the Person in Whose Image You Are Created		Paper roll, crayons, markers, pictures of your kids and of yourself as a child	BCB, p. 23

About
Heritage Builders™

OUR VISION

To build a network of families, churches, and individuals committed to passing a strong family heritage to the next generation and to support one another in that effort.

OUR VALUES

Family—We believe that the traditional, intact family provides the most stable and healthy environment for passing a strong heritage to the next generation, but that non-intact homes can also successfully pass a solid heritage.

Faith—We believe that many of the principles for passing a solid heritage are effective regardless of one's religious tradition, but that the Christian faith provides the only lasting foundation upon which to build a strong family heritage.

Values—We believe that there are certain moral absolutes which govern our world and serve as the foundation upon which a strong heritage should be built, and that the current trend toward value neutrality is unraveling the heritage fabric of future generations.

Church—We believe that all families need a support network and that the local church is the institution of choice for helping families successfully pass a strong heritage to the next generation.

OUR BELIEFS

We embrace the essential tenets of orthodox Christianity as summarized by the National Association of Evangelicals:

1. *We believe the Bible to be the inspired, the only infallible, authoritative Word of God.*

2. *We believe that there is one God, eternally existent in three persons: Father, Son, and Holy Ghost.*

3. *We believe in the deity of our Lord Jesus Christ, in His virgin birth, in His sinless life, in His miracles, in His vicarious and atoning death through His shed blood, in His bodily resurrection, in His ascension to the right hand of the Father, and in His personal return in power and glory.*

4. *We believe that for the salvation of lost and sinful people, regeneration by the Holy Spirit is absolutely essential.*

5. *We believe in the present ministry of the Holy Spirit, by whose indwelling the Christian is enabled to live a godly life.*

6. *We believe in the resurrection of both the saved and the lost; they that are saved unto the resurrection of life and they that are lost unto the resurrection of damnation.*

7. *We believe in the spiritual unity of believers in our Lord Jesus Christ.*

OUR PEOPLE

Heritage Builders™ is lead by a team of family life experts.

Cofounder - J. Otis Ledbetter, Ph.D.
  Married over 25 years to Gail, two grown children, one
    teenager
  Pastor, Chestnut Baptist Church in Clovis, California
  Author - *The Heritage, Family Fragrance, Family
    Traditions*

Cofounder - Kurt Bruner, M.A.
  Married over 12 years to Olivia, three young sons
  Vice President, Focus on the Family Resource Group
  Author - *The Heritage, Family Night Tool Chest* Series

Cofounder - Jim Weidmann
  Married over 15 years to Janet, two sons, two daughters
  Family Night Training Consultant
  Author - *Family Night Tool Chest* Series

Senior Associates - Heritage Builders™ draws upon the collective wisdom of various authors, teachers, and parents who provide resources, motivation, and advice for the heritage-passing process.

BECOME A HERITAGE BUILDER™ IN YOUR COMMUNITY!

We seek to fulfill our mission by sponsoring the following.

HERITAGE BUILDERS™ RESOURCES - Products specifically designed to motivate and assist parents in the heritage-passing process.

HERITAGE WORKSHOP - Using various formats, this seminar teaches attendees the principles and tools for passing a solid heritage, and helps them create a highly practical action plan for doing so.

HERITAGE BUILDERS™ NETWORK - A network of churches which have established an ongoing heritage builder support ministry where families can help families through mutual encouragement and creativity.

HERITAGE BUILDERS™ NEWSLETTER - We provide a forum through which families can share heritage building success stories and tips in our periodic newsletter.

If you are interested in hosting a Heritage Workshop, launching a Heritage Builders™ ministry in your local church, learning about new Heritage Building resources, receiving our newsletter, or becoming a Heritage Builder Associate, contact us by writing, phoning, or visiting our web site.

Heritage Builders Association
c/o Chariot Victor Publishing
4050 Lee Vance View
Colorado Springs, CO 80918
or call: 1-800-528-9489 (7 A.M.– 4:30 P.M. MST)
www.chariotvictor.com
or
www.heritagebuilders.com

HERITAGE BUILDERS™

☐ Please send me a FREE One-Year Subscription to Heritage Builders™ Newsletter.

Name _____

Address _____

City _____ State _____ Zip _____ Phone _____

Church Affiliation _____

E-mail Address _____

Signature _____